Primitivism and Politicking

(An Approach to applying due diligence in corporate leadership roles)

Pramod Kesav N

Notion Press

NOTION PRESS

India. Singapore. Malaysia.

Primitivism and Politicking

Foreword

Acknowledging the fact that we do not have a lot in the English literature in India that may help us give some sense to budding leaders who may be fresh hands and corporate professionals especially when they seem quasi-feudalistic, nationalist, and orthodox in their approaches and support cultural ties as it exists in their numerous societal formations in India with a diverse demand in terms of their followers, colleagues, friends, and pen-pals. In the midst of being a valuable connection it is intended here while using social networking tools so that they remain successful in the emerging economies of today. This is a modest attempt in applying due diligence when such intentions give way to leadership roles in advanced technology companies in the emerging economies.

Good Luck!

Pramod Kesav N

Payikkattu, Kalavamkodam, Cherthala, Alappuzha, Kerala, India.

Contents

Preface

Let us go ahead and see some of the fundamentals that are considered invaluable for an apolitical novice from a foreign country who is culturally and racially, distinct from a region's demography and ponders a little bit on how dangerous their manoeuvring attempts in the Indian corporate world would yield sometimes spectacular results and sometimes utter bleak ones while trying to outperform non-partisan activism amidst professionals in the Indian corporate world who are normally well aware of their background, their organizational culture and their technical knowhow in various subjects.

Under such circumstances, assuming foreign companies prefer local talent from India in various leadership positions, a lot is done usually by the same companies for the proper training and learning upkeep of all its incumbents.

However, apart from the numerous leadership styles that each leader or the incumbents subsume, leadership training can only take a candidate a short distance but a lot of the long haul is to be borne out of sheer determination, experience, some factor of luck as well as performing due diligence by making sure the candidate themselves have not steered away in a course inviting any or all unwanted attention.

So, performing due diligence is a must for any candidate who wants to outperform several things be it competition, competence, updating of leadership skills, leadership qualities that go with the organization or organizations and its culture and above all, the candidate aspiring in a leadership role must have a compelling story or stories to convince the management whether top management in a strategic position or in a tactical direction.

Management of a Company or firm sets minimum expectation from such candidates aspiring for leadership roles or positions and the expectations set for some of them have to do with the candidate acquiring by way of experience or by way of expanding a candidate's own horizon in terms of his or her knowledge in his or her locale, culture, art, society, groups, inter personal communication styles, leadership styles that the candidate is naturally inclined to, etc.

And hence in this work, the importance of Primitivism and Politicking is stressed where the candidate opting to take that approach in leadership roles and decision making is advised to consider the importance of subjects like Humanities, History, Literature, Economics, World Politics, Finance, etc that entirely make up the Leadership continuum in companies that may be in the Public Sector or in the Private Sector in the various emerging economies of the world.

Remember the world has become a small place for us all and our labourers are spread wide in all the emerging economies in various leadership positions and due to the emergence of Artificial Intelligence only in some technical positions, and it is important for us to have an all-round knowledge if certified, better but otherwise also the importance of Knowledge Management cannot be more stressed.

Hope this attempt by me to do due diligence for corporate leadership positions yield the required result and inspire many new incumbents to try for leadership positions in the Indian corporate world.

Good Luck!

Pramod Kesav N

1

Do we need to rewrite Knowledge Management systems?

Do we need to rewrite Knowledge Management systems in support of new Approaches in Leadership training and management?

Do we have to rewrite Knowledge Management systems?

Creative thinkers have for a long time incubated a lot of business ideas and have helped shape up the innovation in technology companies quite often transforming the capital market landscape using at will the economic prowess and political will for favourable market movements.

Robotics on the other hand has evolved in recent times in heaps and bounds to almost matching human capabilities in various segments of human life so much so that peripherally at least human intelligence is challenged in terms of the capabilities that robots can bring to the advanced social structures especially in the western world.

Add to it, the advancements in AI (Artificial Intelligence) which when read alongside Robotic advancements, is like adding fuel to fire, where it is feared that the physical capabilities of humans are at a faster pace getting replaced by robotic gesticulations, alongside the human intelligence quotient increasingly replaced by AI being now believed to be managed by trustworthy power centres.

But it is not soon that this arrangement be overturned risking the skilful living habits of human be replaced by automatic and mechanical ways of living thanks most to living alongside robots and their artificial intelligence centres and is a matter of time when they turn against or in defiance of decisions being taken by human IQ or at a minimum comprehensible social intelligence quotient.

Scores of literature in the last several years have spoken about this, artforms like apocalypse is now increasingly seen to invade human habitat, it is fear that the creative thinkers are faced with, in the innovative industrial segments, what ought to be not thought, whether it is not under the influence of AI or whether AI would leave or save any genuine reasoning with creative thinkers out of creative writing or help them think in the right direction for human survival and not for its destruction.

Robots are invading the human living space, albeit gradually, by conquering corners in the living space in the form of automatic cleaning machines first to concurring decision making in bits and pieces in one form or the other in the professional landscapes to now increasingly in personal avenues of the decision-making landscape.

There used to be at least what is Knowledge Management a subject in the learning curriculum, used to impart the importance of Knowledge systems where it was celebrated the importance of human decision-making when interactions were between humans and tools, with schools of thought like Therbligs favouring human enactments of machines and usually not the other way around.

But that is soon going to change with lightening and faster developments happening in the Robotic space especially in the developed economies questioning the sanity of knowledge and the knowledge base systems forming part of an individual's existence, often not being questioned and often times replaced by some rudimentary AI based decision systems.

For not losing track, now the only way forward is to rely firmly on the familiarity landscape because as individuals one always has the liberty to firmly work on what was acceptable (history) by keeping track of changes in value systems, thought processes and to always keep in check the thought trains, dreams, and the invisible connection points.

To surmise, one needs to ponder whether one's knowledge base system be based out of historical and firmly accepted truths as opposed to part of a degenerating decision tree, whether at all it is not known any existing knowledge system needs replacement.

To second, one also needs to include primitive ways of thought and truths use it as a way to reason against a robotic mishap or an artificial intelligence folly, where it is known that proper human reasoning have always supported human coexistence even when facts and factors deviate out of individual circumstances arising of penury, prejudice, neglect, etc.

Hence it is urged to second and support Primitivism and Politicking as an Approach in Leadership Management while doing due diligence studies in the context when one considers leadership positions in an AI based company so that human values are cherished and pure mechanical, automated ways of thinking are challenged and avoided in any advanced technology situations.

We do not realize even today that at some level, we are at war with the robots. Ultimately a sound, morally right, and peaceful war need to be fought with them where it is the need of the hour to make sure human intelligence prevails over the fast pace and ruthless artificial ones.

2

Primitivism in the USA

Let us first take a look at how difficult it is to be a believer in Primitivism and any policies that may emerge from it, be it in the normal course of living or for specific purposes in the day to day living.

Primitivism (Primitive Activism) is highly problematic, problems were identified earlier in the 1st Century AD, in forms it was revealed much later in plots invented by New Harlem writers and in the form of alternate plots by Renaissance writers.

In the case of Dramatic gestures, the Religious Ministries always referred the Concerned lots to those Artists as to what goes on with them while doing caricatures of African American voices and folk traditions in shows.

For doing African American roles in plays, voice Appropriation is concerned with gender and consciousness issues including Mel-Angtha stains or G stains which are accurate usages of African American voice forms, despite an existing Joyce Representation on female consciousness.

Modernism always put to test any literary form and expression, as exemplified by Ezra Pound's maxim for anything but renaissance.

This literary movement was driven by a deliberate and conscious desire to overturn traditional modes of representation and express the new sensibilities of the time.

As far as possible, a post-modernist and an apolitical runner should move away from any such attempts if that person believes in true primitivism as an element to be inculcated into his politicking attempts by considering the acute combinations of dramaticism, racism, and post modernism in all its avenues.

Modernist dialect literature is also always concerned with Voice Appropriation. Alan Locke the modernist welcomed Enthusiasm for African Art.

The usage of Distinct in Class Appropriation and Colonialism in the post-colonial period shows distinct and different European notion of Class Appropriation. According to Kenneth-Coult Smith in his General Observations and in his shows has always emphatically stated that Appropriation is in fact Black treatment by which what he meant is treating anybody the same way a black person is treated in the USA.

In Harris Rabbit stories the concerned always added to the Religious Orders in the Ministries. The Judgment after all was on the Artist's use of the other culture and caricature as well as on the matters of interpretation that was anyway leading most of the translators to go in an out of job status.

During those days, one should not forget the fact that Goethe's (in primitive activism Southe's) influence was on the Commentaries in that regard.

3

An Immigrant of the World in America

There is a saying from some eminent person that immigrants of the world are having an unusual day in North America to indicate that all or everybody in the new world (America) is an immigrant when you go through the family trap with a gap of a few generations or a staunch migrant's drive resulting in the need for an imminent one in their country, all decided at a time at the Immigration Desk at the Port of Entry in North America.

For an apolitical activist, may be the immigration desk in North America might have skilfully prepared a few questionnaires, answering them properly may get them the much-anticipated entry, answering those questions in an unsatisfactory tone may also invite rejections which would mean they would be sent back to their home country by the immigration desk.

So, my favourite encounter at the immigration desk in New York City in the new millennia went like this.

Straight drive, procrastinate the unassuming visitor at the Inspection kiosk. I want to head straight towards the Judicial House, a Birch House amongst many in Fairfax, Virginia, the seat of unparalleled Justice Systems. Can you show me the way? Yes, I would, a confident reply from the Immigration official got me the go ahead to an Introspection room for further interviews for the lawful resident.

Next, please, an impatient Law Enforcement. Oh Yes, I get a go-ahead to see the Golden bright-edge and the castles that go beyond a ferry in the Pacific sea. Yes, the green channel please, the inspector shows him the welcome without holding a placard.

Next? goes the Law Enforcement. I am Green-lander with a hawkish accent. On a business visa, yes sir how may I help you?

This and more from the Immigration Desk at the Port of Entry are routine at best for most travellers.

The other day quite a bit was heard of racism and the Brown v Topeka… How long is going to be the wait? Some hint at Charlottesville. Some more hint at conventions…

To restate some, for renewing a harmful Residence, the process goes on for decades, cries the harbinger, enough is enough now it is all green for continental favouritism and cheapest reaches. No, the Immigration Process is no problem. The Educated slapped already at a back seat. Questioned? yes; when do we see Immigrant laws of those impoverished uneducated working-class Conquistadors? When do we ever beat the odds for a unified community at best in the land of Immigrants? When do we see the Immigrant laws rewritten again for better days ahead for those Impoverished Uneducated working-class Immigrants? Fingers Crossed!

A few moments of delay proved nothing.

Thankfully, it was told to me that the apolitical activism was shown a big welcome in NYC in the new millennium!

4

Apolitical Long Island (A District 133)

The following Scheme on a High-class bill is Farm Labour Bill is Central and explores activism amidst psycho traumatic worries, ends up in environmental activism, subsidies, and frugal apolitical means mostly culminates in a post on Haunting thoughts!

Tunnel Games in Railroad

The railroad is where the seemingly innocent activism is shot and buried.

Tunnel games in Staten Island go on and is where very few hurry to pose alongside the art "Hang Themselves" are immediately ushered away from the tracks, the tracks situated right alongside transponders and the electrified railroads besides the fields indeed.

Rest assured, the whimsical guards will sure beat the tracks, to mention the woman on tracks is a metaphor unless the following guards are on a search for her secret mate, a Siberian Cat who wishes for a narrow escape away from the railroads into the Farm.

The mention of shortlisted candidates almost always gives up on the mandate for her secret mate, the cat, and the secret mate gives a narrow escape to the victim considering, the following facts.

What are those facts?

It is that near Staten Island, there is Assembly District 133, where Tunnel games always go on in fields and in the Memorial Bridge.

Also, the Tunnel games go on near the Transponders for the Silverline train service where the Roominess of the Siberian cat ends up in a feeling that transforms threats into instant captive's activism and ends up in beings watching the predator exercises for a Dream Catcher, snatcher, and a Cannibal.

The ill effects and social implications of a Marjorie is not one of Fragmentation, defined otherwise is thought in terms of a psychological term that stands for assuming the ill-effects from someone else's activities, dreams, experience with Tirade and Toys that are on the levels of systemic failures.

The Threat remains in unique preservations, and concerns the exposure in extempore shows, reveals failure of Federal systems, Individual rights, systemic abuses on Protectionism, constitutionalism, and civil rights.

After all of these, there exists the so-called personality conflicts, personality preferences so on and so forth.

Adieu.

5

A Detainee of the Reindeer's Force
(Context of Double Speak in usage)

Double Speak is shying away from harsh realities as far as its usual usages go, in a rhetoric it most often must convey spoken languages amplifying evasive euphemisms and in manifestations of coward but awkward polite conversations.

Reindeer's force under the then Mayor of NYC, Mr. Rudy Giuliani had to be in full alert and its good usage emancipates from the fact that anybody who revisited the last decade of the twentieth century New York City might have had to deal with an influx of Grenadians and a brutal onslaught of the underworld kingpins.

The emphasis here is on the brutal force usages, it did not a bit cleanse the exteriors on the streets in NYC - 42nd street in particular it was a nightmare for many – subway riders were like leaping frogs – to get free from the misty moistures that lingered quite a bit on the most-tidy streets – in revelation the tidiest of all streets.

Despite Reindeer's force was very much a curse in disguise, without them, the Big Apple might have taken the short breadth and see the shallow brighter dwellers on streets amass greatest wealth in terms of Ripe Mangoes and the rich red tomatoes.

Night life would have been an existential remaking of the Great Awakening of the 1930s where the shops had plenty to offer for anybody with a dream, at times refuting to make some more culpable of living dreams and not for those who were living with a dream.

And amongst that cadre were a few more who appreciated Double Speak and were acting detainee in the Reindeer's force.

6

Usual Rock n Roll, R&B Band Reviews in Philadelphia

Not quite recently on a trip from Philly (Philadelphia), all were reminded of the Rock band favourite Boyz Band, a local band in Philadelphia whose next few lines were heard as, making advancement to the second person You by handing over rose petals and thorns.

Nice song, well heard, the amusements and adulations were very many from the spectators inside the vehicle, though the even spacing and congestive posture did demand an action of swing to convey that much but since it was scantly on the first person I or mine; all I could do was to have scarcely enjoyed it.

It sure had the undivided attention of the thinking tanks from riverside bounties and on galloping acts in drags and riches.

Some were of the opinion that the band did not lose much, in terms of their promise to become a Men's band and in terms of their overtures in throwing the rose petals on ground. There was also nothing smashingly reverberating out of the Waterfalls movement and nothing whatsoever heard about the policy of Accommodation-a-l-i-s-m.

The elites were already drawing the swords and close to beating down the Hotchkiss brand-wagon bush (not to be reminded of hearing voice from the band members) when more felt the zigzag-zoo movements of the vehicle was not a clear attempt to cleanse them of the rainbow lines and to forever downplay the rudimentary dialog.

At that moment, one could only throw oneself into the vivid mannerisms and sloppy imaginations resulting from a guide's best attempts to calm down the situation.

It is genuinely agreed upon that as a community many have rode past the covenants of busing and many have walked thus far beyond the stripes and strides …

Yes, in some sense walking out of the vehicle near a gas station (petrol bunk) helped.

Walking alone, several thoughts ran through the mind, the mind of endless possibilities.

A sudden thought and impression were that things have so far worked in a certain manner for generations, does not mean that the hard binding Walkers and Pokers have to be completely forgotten, important it is to have earned their trust and then a place amongst the first of equals rather than walk aimlessly literally as a matter of pride.

Stripping of sorts has always happened whether in Cheyenne or in Pea Ridge. It was way far easier for the European settlers to first modernize the fierce trading weaponry outpost of Americans or American Indians and then later to have disarmed them in deal weaponry and in dreary Camps at the fathomable outposts like Pine Ridge and Red Clouds.

The common thoughts remained and troubled the self quite a bit!

Who is going to have to see a Bigfoot or a Buffalo Bill especially when it is painted as an epitome of scary, avenging characters in those Halliday movies!

Who is going to walk that extra step to not outlandishly buy presents from forgotten American Indian outposts?

So, for the Boyz band, it is a fabulous crowd indeed and fewer than more have matured into the Men's club thinking way beyond the Rose petals and of the adamant Carpets that always advance the much-awaited welcome.

"Welcome", some was heard singing to the formidable paths that lead to another and their other accoutrements; that they have disembarked on a journey as the best of the Ten's Creed, another local band and "welcome "again for the better of the illustrations though occasionally on moon walks and the pathway beyond.

This was as if I had dreamt up the whole sequence, it was too good to be true!

I was thinking where was the car which I was in, where was the hydrant that left a dent on the car which was mine, where was the blind who was walking on the sidewalk with the same stick who was now howling and waving.

Take care, somebody seemed to have shouted at thyself from a distance, as if their vehicle seemed to have made a graceful exit.

7

Twenty seconds of a Sabbatical

Sabbatical in actual American English translates or indicates holidays. Now we are here not to go into the merits of calling holidays for an extended period as a sabbatical but it means what it means.

There also the favourite quotes remain!

"For a Regent most Communion is unilateral"

"Bilateral-ism is always subjects between equal powers"

"To run for a public office generally lateral knowledge should not undermine the populist altitudes in Lateral-ism"

But what was interesting was a train journey in Amtrak train that I would like to quote which extended from New Brunswick in New Jersey to Embarcadero in California, roughly a week, actually a four-day tour, a sabbatical is a real stretch but let's put it that way.

Now what stole the show was a train and a leader, for convenience lets call the train the Amtrak Zephyr.

A few years later a millennium is when some people try their luck at embarking on a train journey from Chicago in Illinois to Embarcadero in California with the laid-back attitude of the West Coast to bully the street side smirks of the East coast of US.

In a train the overtures become the much more compartmental attitudes in a cabin car and crew with transparent roof in a bogie providing ultimatums and views of stellar propositions to its Ecclesiastic prodigy and performance artists. The journey easily extends a full sabbatical roughly a week taking the traveller through the Midwest, Midland prairies, the Dakotas and deserts finally arriving in the West Coast on its way from Chicago.

From then on, there are cabs and ferries available that gets the go ahead towards the city of San Francisco.

Disembarking the train, one is imaginative immediately of the solo passenger, a Teachout who was profusely proud for, a day of Devotion in an year and hopelessly dependent on the best variety breweries and wines.

Like in a normal conversation, what went interesting was the sort of questions that was in store when somebody uttered the word Law or the lack of it in corporate governance. The response to it was largely supportive of the genuine causes of the caged, be it a juvenile victim, first time defence, chargeable indictments on a sidewalk or a traffic violation or ticket.

Barnacles and Shells were an ideological fight and so were the absurd proportions of the safety concerns in re-inducting the caged-bird in corporate-houses with the state having to have to spent quite a bit on surveillance and to bear the consequences of the loud boisterous shouts and liberty slogans.

Besides that, out of the utterance, there was a promise made for a lot of inventive and interesting stuffs like Paganism, Altruism, Vulture-ism, Vocational Hunt, and Drama.

Twenty seconds normally second not an extra moment more in these verbatim travelogues.

Bye!

8

One day of Theatres and Plays in the San Francisco Circuit

(Castle Games)

An activist whether political or apolitical should have a proper cause for activism by gathering political consensus among their supporters by looking at issues as they are and not digressing it in terms of financial and benefits drawn out of art, that may accrue as a result of conducting a series of Concerts that was originally planned on Pier 13 in the San Francisco Quay or Bay.

The issues may be just about anything and everything from those that may emerge out of not leading a disciplined life to hitting the extremities of being an extrovert and a flirt.

That evening in Pier 13 in San Francisco Bay, it was conveyed to everybody that Yeats Edmond Goose's financial pensions led to the Constitutional Crisis at the Concert held on 1910, which are Stages set near Pier 13 named Concert 1910, 1929...

CG Code was required but it was interpreted that the two letters that were said to have come from Yeats demanded an Apology from Goose!

At Coole Park the Fay brothers were ousted! Yeats John Quinn's current mistress, a Cathleen Nesbitt an actress and spy took care of the Financial Crisis and was thought to have gotten involved in the making of the Letters of Yeats.

In defence of CN, Yeats used to write for the Concert on 1929 at Coole Park. There, John Quinn felt like embracing Irish boys and girls and Synge thought wearing a Green helmet was better.

At Castle games, a Stage set near Pier 13, the Lady Layard in Venice dreamt of Air and Heir at Compass points, but someone had to awaken her to thwart the tipsy for her to think it was not at a gun point.

Castle Ground weekly meetings were also getting held at the landlord's palace for which they needed two mermaids to work on German Accents until Queen Alexandria the then Empress of Russia proclaimed and said, "Yeats would not meet Coole on a visit to Dunsany Castle".

Yeats met with his sisters in O'Connell street and said he would write, "King of Cats" and would collect the work in 8 volumes from A H Bullen at the Shakespeare Head Press.

The following arguments held in favour of Yeats' Letters and check collections were made for the Agreements and to place a claim on Wyndham Land.

That John Shaw Taylor did the Act, that which was Wyndham Land Act was a stupid show depicting the Conservative Policy of killing the Home Rule; the Act also screened the Career of Hugh Lane who was the Picture Dealer and was found to be destroyed through mythologies important to Yeats.

The counter defence did notice the statements in which it was said that Miss Horniman stopped the subsidiary checks that were given to by Yeats.

That Yeats did confirm that he spent every summer at Coole Park until 1912 started in a Stage near Pier 13.

Some conclusions were difficult but many understood they cannot be easily drawn.

And accordingly, Horniman was always opinionated. Yeats always supported Molly All Good. Mark and Cuchulain who were Yeats's alter ego amongst George Mure were among the ones who go against Synge.

George Mure fakes the name day after day and begins to start stealing for which he is sentenced to 10 years in imprisonment in Dublin and moves to Dublin in Concert 1911.

At Britannica, the old lady AE is rumoured to be the Author of the Parody, Cathleen is in Hooligan set in a stage in a makeshift near the Pier 13.

Sien Fein is there everywhere in the newspaper.

The Playboy debates gave bad terms to AE Synge. AE thinks GM is saving satin for Church and Welby.

In the end E Nia-u-self becomes consulting lawyers.

9

Hopi, a new hop to your communication style

There exists no relationship between ethnic groups, what exist is a relationship between their Languages, Culture, and a thought.

Well, to come to the point…

Now is the perfect time for me to reveal some hidden secrets in me. Yes, you guessed it right, my communication style which I myself was not aware of. It is like opening the 4th pane of the Johari window to reveal secrets of myself, which I myself don't know and so is not known also to You the second subject and They the third subjects.

I always thought I was very analytical.

But when I took some of the self-assessment questionnaire available in the market, it had a different viewpoint on me based on the inputs that I provided.

Well, they thought I was more Direct, which is an English Communication style which is decisive, competitive, independent, and confident and then I was also initiating, which would mean I was sociable, enthusiastic, energetic, and fun loving.

They also rated me to bear a supportive style and thought I was very calm, approachable, sincere, and gentle.

Also, I was somewhere Analytical, where they thought I may be precise, exact, and logical.

Now let us leave all the Market Ratings aside, I know it is really hard for anybody to glue themselves to a particular communication style but here we are a mix of different communication styles which helps us go well, mingling, mixing as well as be a true product of the Communicating Diversity.

But you see I had also my reservations too in a typical discussion on communication style.

My interest was to know how easy it is for a non-native speaker of English like me influence a typical native speaker of English, be it on an individual basis or be it in a social, cultural, or in their societal framework.

I thought I will share with you, my findings.

So, in order to do that we should first understand what is Linguistic relativity or linguistic determination?

To reach linguistic relativity, it is all about how a particular language influences the reality around us.

To reach linguistic determination, it is about language and its structure limiting human knowledge and the human thought process.

In short it says a one-to-one translation of any foreign language be it Indo Aryan or Dravidian language to English is somewhat difficult.

And if that is the case, what is most difficult is a one-to-one translation from a language called Hopi to English.

What is Hopi?

Hopi well is a Native American language spoken in North America.

Western languages and most Indo Aryan or Dravidian languages view time as a flowing river carrying us through the present, away from past and to the future.

But Native Americans who speak Hopi has no concept of this. For them, or for the Hopi language speakers, there is no present, past or future tense. They simply divide the world into manifested and unmanifested domains.

The manifested domain consists of the physical universe including present, immediate past and the future and unmanifested domain consists of remote past, future and the world of dreams, thoughts, desires, and life forces.

Simply put they follow phases of moon and movements of sun...

And hence, the Native speakers of Hopi language in America had real difficulty adapting to English speaking world in particular when they were asked to perform a particular job on time or to be on time for a particular job.

So let us from now on, don't sympathize with the Hopi language speakers in North America, understand that their differences with the English-speaking world is manifested in well-known Hypothesis like the Sapir-Whorf hypothesis, a discussion on that may not be imminent for us here but may be taken up in a subsequent session.

Ciao.

10

Insurance Fraud revealed in the Practice of Firm Audit

A firm shall be always duty bound, responsible and responsive to its customers whether the customers are stakeholders in the firm, clients of the firm or even other employee of the firm it is serving at its best.

Insurance services should be handled with utmost care and precaution in the modern-day firm though in very many working places or offices offer modest accommodations and frailest policies within the confines of a Learning Organization based in Virginia, USA.

Employee insurance policies are cohesive and unified measures of social assurance or coverage extended to a firm's employee according to an Insurance Act enforceable at the location of the place of work, protecting the Employee from unforeseen circumstances such as sickness, disablement etc.

It is unfortunate to see these very avoidable unforeseen circumstances often avoided by the Employee, going unnoticed causing it to harm the very existence of the Employee by fraudster Insurance Consultants who file Fraudulent Insurance Policy on behalf of the Employee and then go on charging for Established Anomaly Procedures.

To say the least in the learning organization this story seems to have happened! Any reasonable educated Insurance Consultant knows which types of policies are to be applied whenever an Employee of the Firm applies for insurance; granted there may be typographical flaws while deciding upon Life Coverage Premium, Premium Adjustment rates, etc. But in the Learning organization, however, quite on the contrary and out of the ordinary, out of the unexpected seems to have happened!

The fraud is more revealing when the Insurance Policy of the Employee upon examination, is recorded to have contained the clauses from, Clauses in Good Faith of an Underwriting Program or an Underwriting Policy for Insurance taken by the Company to cover up unsubscribed or under-subscribed lots of shares which is offered for bidding.

Rest of the questions posed many conundrums and objective assessments to the Consultant who then seemed to have "helped" the Company to robustly make its processes Fault Effective and Magnanimously Extensive.

The Employee's liabilities sky rocketed because of the Insurance Policy Changes more than the Concern's Liability to an Unsubscribed Debenture Plan and the premiums were beyond over-harm for any Consenting Employee in the crucial circumstances.

Some might call these moves preposterous; some might unravel the Insurance Process followed in the Firm by immediately employing an Audit Firm.

In this case, we believe necessary disciplinary actions are taken by the firm and an appropriate Industrial Audit may have settled the score that aroused out of the situations.

For a fact, it is true that Insurance Fraud exists from the time the Insurance business progressed in the Commercial Industry ...

Insurance claims are rising and follow a pattern on a case-by-case basis where the Insurance companies are said to have lost millions as a result of fraud or misrepresentation.

According to Coalition against Fraud, the numbers of insurance fraud are staggering and said to make up ten percent Property

Severity Insurance loss and an equal amount in adjustment loss and expenses. The State has so far come strong with the devising of anti-fraud measures where in, in the US alone there are about forty-eight states making Insurance Fraudulent activities, a Specific Crime.

In most of the states in US, there exist what is called as Fraud Bureau that looks into insurance fraud cases and transactions reported or brought to its attention with immediate effect.

The Cross over Schemes in Fraudulent Plots are increasingly getting more complex because it involves multiple industries and the Investigation has revealed Schemes of Higher concerns such as in Identity theft, Hacking, Employee Agents, and Fraudulent Claims.

Frauds cost more than five to ten percent of claims in the US and Canada.

Nearly one third insurance companies say as high as twenty percent costs are lost in Personal-Property Fraud, Auto-Insurance Claims, and Activation of Organized Crime Rings.

Some of the acts that prevent Fraudulent Insurance Activities include Whistle-blowing Federal False Claims Act where the FCA alone can lead any of the False Claims making it illegal and a Criminal Charge.

Overall, in the highly specialized and intricate Insurance Business Industry, the Committees like the Whistle-blower Committee shall be extremely wary and watchful of Insurance Frauds taking place in the Insurance Space and supplement the workforce with Specialized Personals or Committed Inspectors and Insurance Contractors who are Ethical and Honest and have an unbeaten track record of non-shoddy workmanship and un-exploitation of the Employee.

11

The Irish Potato Blight of 1845

It is not exactly known when potatoes were introduced in Ireland.

Many believe it happened sometime in 1600 when a ship arrived from Spain with a few tonnes of potatoes.

For many years, Europeans believed that potatoes belonged to a poisonous breed.

That changed with Ms. Marie Antoinette when she wore potato blossoms on her hair, and it suddenly became a novelty in the entire Europe.

By the 1700s, the dietary value of potatoes was discovered and most Monarchs in Europe wanted it to be planted in the entire Europe.

By 1800, most of the Irish population became dependent on potatoes as a staple diet.

It was believed that about six pounds of potatoes were consumed by an Irish farmer daily and the potatoes were stored in the winter season and were even fed to the livestock.

Before Potato Blight struck Ireland, overpopulation was a main concern of Ireland.

During 1840, the population of Ireland tripled from 3 million people to nine million.

Potatoes were blamed for this ubiquitous increase in the Irish population since they contained all the nutrients that a person needed for survival.

In 1845, Potato Blight, or the destruction of potatoes happened in Ireland.

At first, they thought, the potato blight was caused by static energy or railroad smoke, even volcanoes were blamed for it.

But later it turned out that potatoes were affected by a fungal disease that originated in Mexico. Through ships, it reached Ireland and caused the Potato Blight of 1845 in Ireland.

After the failed crop in 1845, the population of Ireland was reduced to a quarter.

The reason for the decline in the Irish Population was not only because of the Potato Famine but it was chiefly because of the British Tenure system and the inadequate policies that were taken by the British people towards Ireland.

Now it is time to look at some more Irish history.

Following the Napoleonic wars in 1815, the English were only interested in primary land holdings and ownership, and they started extracting resources from Ireland, charging expensive rent, and collecting taxes from the Irish people.

During those times, the Protestant landlords from England owned 95% of the Irish land, that got divided amongst them.

This forced the Irish people to move to less fertile land where the food was scarce and often not enough for the floating Irish population.

This decimated the Irish population.

It is hence a fact that many of the effects of the Irish potato famine are still evident in Ireland in the form of homes that were evacuated by absentee landlords that still sit in Irish hills and taverns, abandoned.

Several Irish people even today carry greater animosity towards the British (English) for not having left them a proper legal code, that might have helped put their interests before the British political establishments.

Summarizing, the Irish potato blight haunts the Irish people even today, no lesser is their concerns in North America, where most of them have migrated and remain there as landlords.

12

A Demographic Bait
(A half-hearted criticism of a Play in the Making)

Life of an English elite is always celebrated throughout, at the backdrop of the English countryside in various streams of literary works, often exemplifying characters and their emotional facets, leadership qualities, emotional quotients and very rarely in a retiree's melancholy.

Now is an opportunity to explore one, especially when one condescends the transitory nature of world politics, where with an acute appreciation lies the Anglican real public whenever they are informed of unification attempts of the North American Empire on one side, where on the other side renowned role models of the crown's political leadership resort to blame games, inter-continental politics, in reality, rendering some of English elites jobless and many of the others clueless.

While analysing the utopian play, A Demographic Bait, one is always inspired to find out the invisible dots that connect the lives of average (North) Americans, enjoying two square meals a day, to find their daily earnings spread thin for a daily stay at a cosy and comfortable inn.

But in this anecdote, since we are talking about a fallen angel from political stardom in North America, we try to paint a form of criticism based on the utopian play theme, "A Demographic Bait" and try to picture the character by exemplifying the life of an English Elite from British North America where the subject transforms his own life from a hefty political disorder to leading an average North American life in blues and under the rainbow banner.

But one cannot always assume that these Satirical anecdotes working to formalize a play, may not end up in, political sensationalism, even though it addresses privileges and perceptions in powerful Acts, a natural biproduct of formalizations in a play, even when the utopian play theme is titled, A Demographic Bait.

Had it been that the characters were from British North America faring the intolerable acts of the Quebec province, or in short, natives from the US state Indiana, modest revivals could have been attempted as was what was supposed to be in Izaak Walton's work which may be "The Compleat Angler" or the limitless bounties during those days, where there was some promise that it was supposed to end up in creating a complete assortment of activities, including activities for writing, singing, dancing and the play!

But introspecting the content, one is made to think in the other way.

While introspecting more the contents of the play, A Demographic Bait, one goes adamantly vicious in revealing the structure of the hopeless ethnic vote markets in North America that inherently wishes a rescue attempt of the hopeless apolitical characters who are seeking an exit from active politicism by sparing nobody including Pirates in the Caribbean to the trading American Indian in the Reservation areas because a causation felt political apathy at the expense of a third world idealism.

Third class schematics were also drawn not at all to attract eagles and vultures but to draw adherence to the genre of apolitical hatred that was released in instalments to sympathize the conclusion of the section, Homeland Confederations.

When asked, what in the world a confederation has, the quick wit replies and takes out the fear of fireman and cops, while attempting the norm calls and the dress code of night life participation and how to adeptly master, the skills of going along with a bunch of losers in real life.

This more or less have suggested that, there a non-conjugal alliance (dating) was very much in scope between courteous singles under the auspicious of whatever Confederation that was mentioned in the play, A Demographic Bait, the intent is what needs to be questioned, and what needs to be examined is the phrase and the usage of the phrase, "in the context of Homeland Confederations", in having used political activism to include night life activities and participation in North America.

So, the general public on the other hand enduring these ordeals of difficulty and bear from such acts by the Englishman who may be a politician, should ask the real question and that is, What was the Demographic bait and not who was the bait?

The prognosis from the play then is that, this without a doubt has left the concurring English man who may be a politician in a North American political setup feel a state of political freedom, now wants to resign and retire in a lucid green landscape by waving the sign of peace and tranquillity in lush meadows and who knows might have also wanted participation in an underwater expedition.

Agreed, most of the English elites' resort to the jobless markets of Animal Control, Underwater navigation, Gun Control, and the Casino Business as a last resort, but some at the behest of political stardom feeling quite let down now attempt an aspiring call to all these activities is at the same time a namesake loss to inter-continental politics and a call-in for the competence of many leading a peaceful retiree's life.

In plain words, (British) North America is where the English leads a retired life and it is not a place where there is a heavy demand for high labour and skilled work, as most others think. It is retiree's paradise.

Noting this, it is also a fact that any demographic activity does not ideally reflect this to have considered the entire North American empire to be a labour powerhouse.

And in essence, the usage of Demographic data is never to be used as a bait is a very commonplace knowledge.

So, adios, bravo and fringe benefactor, from the abode of Gaulish retreats in North America for being a cheerful party wig, and let us hope your literary work, A Demographic Bait cheer up countless leaders and sprout bountiful envy upon cheerless larks.

13

A Homeless and Asylum seeker Bob in San Francisco City

A Bob is colloquial (slang) used to refer to a British Shilling coin and hence in the present time this article refers to what in general an acquirer (by the name of a Bob) of a British Shilling has when he is given as an Alm, a British Shilling which is no good other than meeting means for a Bob-Ben and an Uncle Sam...

At first sight, Bob may not have thought about its significance, for occupying a cabin meant for the security guard, at the asylum's reception area, let alone, extend the bald ribaldry sketches, as a gesture of welcoming residents, to the premises of a confined mesh up.

On second thoughts, he may have reminded us, of an overcrowded metropolis, that stood outside, knowing nothing of Medicare facilities, and about planned healthcare, that went berserk at the fragmented thoughts of a few challenged ones, who once upon a time belonged to the well adorned social class.

Bob says he likes to watch TV in his free time, from a silent quarter, far away from the Faraday cage, inviting as little attention from the asylum wanderers of whom he says, some are businessmen, and some of whom are from the glorious industries.

Now let us go in retrospective that is going back a few decades, when it was clear what it was for a Bob who was constantly living the life of a homeless in the lesser-known streets of San Francisco City.

For a Bob, this universal truth held true. That is, competing medical resurgences find compelling reasons, enough to push malevolent symptoms of homelessness, some head towards as detached asylum seekers, leaving the sycophancy at the doorsteps of stags and riches.

That one day, Bob exactly cannot remember the decisions that one day, what prompted him to take the first steps out of a recovery bed, that made him realize of imminent idiosyncrasies on liquids, than-of an immediate one waiting at the half open sidewalk.

The day he was an Asylum seeker, he remembered about the nightingale or caretaker, who was apprehensive of the well bloomed floors and the mirror like finish of decorated tiles, making the ornamental design an absolute must, for transparent orders and odourless wines.

With a pronounced indifference to dominating attitudes, the nightingale routinely delivers lecturers on table etiquette and manners, that ought to exist before taking medication, that are samples of conceptual drugs to control cub instincts and weed makeovers.

On Blue grass and Red Herrings cravings, Bob felt flamboyant affluence of oratory dementia, that went on affecting him and a few patients, had nothing at all to do with insurance cycles conforming to recuperated aspects and pragmatic views.

Now let us envision what burdens are carried or borne out by a Bob, the homeless as he says is mainly ELISA the Medical Kit, who is now posing as another Asylum Seeker in the San Francisco Asylum.

In Bob it may have meant guts to overcome depressive but elusive outbursts, quite often of eagerness and uncertainty of homeless burdens, make him unsure of repetitive calls from sequestered quarters, proclaiming separations, settlements, shut doors, and a policy.

Rendezvous, doesn't it feel better? cries Eliza, an asylum seeker from next door, when the distorted alphabets lie wonderfully crushed with its deformities and analogies, in retrospective indicating quagmire symptoms emerge as an analogy, or riddle for the Framers.

So, here we are let known that ELISA medical kit which was in asylum out of scarcity is now seen to getting completely exhausted in San Francisco City. So also, we are told that the ELISA medical kit is no more available and is no more required in San Francisco City posing a question to those wanting it just because they met Bob, the acquirer of the British Shilling.

Let go the inhibitions, in a marble, tombstone, or the bulge brackets, let us also hope Bob does not strike any more characters off but do scrutinize but let go the ones who were once trapped by him for want of angel (funds), shelter (garage), and a winning idea.

These days it is also known that the same Bob lives on in the San Francisco City holding dear that British Shilling that was given as an Alm to him on decorated tiles and as a marble, that some may worth cherishing may be a century later…

14

Organizational Development and Industrial Relations at Cross Roads

Organizational Development (OD) and Industrial Relations (IR) in many ways are complementary subjects in MBA studies in the Human Resource Management stream, even-though the Approach followed by each of the subjects in Academia is contrasting, OD following a Management Approach whereas Industrial Relations is chiefly an Administrative Approach to Problem Solving.

Reasons why Industrial Relations is Shrinking

First in academia, Industrial Relations which was introduced by John R Commons in the University of Wisconsin in 1920, is threatened by the emergence of Mainstream Economics and Organizational behaviour on one side, and by the effects of Post Modernism on the other side.

Second, IR is shrinking in Policy Making Circles because Trade Unionism in itself is marginalized as well as kept outside of Mainstream business.

In the Indian scenario, it may also be or partly because of the diminishing interest of the role played by the Government in Tripartite Bodies with dynamic market condition, performance-based wage system as well as resource pool availability scenario prevalent in today's extremely competitive market landscape.

Group Dynamics and Planned Change in Organizational Development

OD has evolved many folds from the time it was introduced in the early 1950s to the present time. Keeping its roots well immersed in Group Dynamics and Planned Change, the field of

OD is based on the following subjects such as, psychology, sociology, anthropology, systems theory, and organizational behaviour.

Consultants who are trained in Organizational Behaviour become OD Practitioners with underlying knowledge of Behavioural Sciences.

There exist two major goals of Organizational Development and are Improvement and Teaching. What it improves is functions of Teams, Individuals, and Organizations and whom it teaches is Organizational Members so that they improve their own functioning.

In essence, where-ever Organizational Members, Teams, and Individuals do not realize their full potential, OD can help improve the situation.

Organizational Development is defined as a planned effort that is organization wide and managed from the top increasing effectiveness and health through planned interventions in the organizational process using behavioural science knowledge (Bechard).

Organizational Development is also defined as a response to change a complex educational strategy, beliefs, attitudes, values, structure of organization in a way making the organizational adapt to changing markets, technologies, and challenges.

Systematic Organizational Development is a mix of different approaches of which, the prominent ones are Laboratory Training, Survey Research and Feedback, Action Research Method and Tavistock's Socio-Technical and Socio-Clinical Approaches.

The Laboratory Training Approach started in New Britain, Connecticut, in the premises of State Teacher's College involving participant's own actions and group dynamics. When Feedback was introduced by scholars like Kurt Lewin, this approach moulded into T-Group Training for group members and group leaders, with additional awareness creation and focus on leadership processes.

In Survey Research and Feedback, the participating activities under this approach was planned and executed in Survey Research Centre in the University of Michigan. This Approach discovered Needs, Feelings, and Attitudes of Employees of an Organization and dealt with Human Relations as a whole.

Effective tools that were used in activities spanning this Approach are intensive Group Discussions, Procedures for utilizing Results of an Employee Questionnaire where survey is seen as an effective tool in introducing positive changes in the organization. The Reports collected during this activity is fed-back to management and to the Employees. Any serious employee concerns or attitude is an area for Organizational Development Problem Solving.

In Action Research Model and Organizational Development, the essentials are same and are action oriented, data based, calls for close cooperation between insider and outsider and are both problem-solving social interventions.

Sample Interventions in this regard were Gavin's Survey Feedback Program conducted in a mine and a massive Organizational Development Program conducted in a Finnish Banking Group to gain knowledge on how the OD Program was implemented in 80 largest banks in a 270 plus Banking System (REMA).

According to Tavistock Approach, the study was undertaken in University of South California and was associated with mostly socio-technical changes.

The attempts there created a better fit amongst technologies, structure, and social interactions of a particular production unit in a Mine, Factory, or an Office.

In other words, Socio Technical Research was about Restructuring involving Redesign of Work Systems, Total Quality, Self-selected Work Teams, and Reengineering.

Fundamentally, what drove OD was behavioural science, convergence tactics which was done by mending ways so that organization wide there was concurrence of strategic directions, quite often taken at a high level owe to changing market conditions, etc.

For Industrial Relations, the central theme were conflicts emerging out of employee dissatisfaction over benefits given to them including wages, pay, bonus, leave sanctioned, office facilities like creche, etc that were attempted to be resolved in a tripartite arrangement, involving government, employers and employee unions. To say, the least about Industrial Relations a a subject, it can be definitely said that the subject was quite reflexive of socialist economics approach and not capitalistic market-based approach.

Hence, it can be surmised that Organizational Development caters to Markets and Capitalist/Market Economy whereas Industrial Relations cater to Public and Social/Socialist/Mixed Economy.

15

Role of Societal Conditions in IR and OD

It is imperative to think and style the contributions made by societies in whose favour persons have transformed themselves to personalities to becoming corporeal citizens in every aspect to not lose sight of Directive Policies in a different subject nor be viciously following an institution's staunch lack of social responsibilities.

Hence, Social Responsibilities range higher in nominal terms for any Employee, social reverberance can only be understood by taking up a focused look into societies in which a corporate body functions as well as the societal conditions attached hence off.

Society in general benefits from Industrial Relations by achieving the given objectives, primarily, Rights of an individual, Equality of Opportunity, a living wage, and a work life balance.

Rights of an Individual: Industrial Relations seem to protect the rights of an individual through its different processes and channels. This would mean, even for an intermittently unemployed youth, it works in such a way that it protects him, by lobbying on his behalf, fights for his rights to be respected, even when he unconditionally enters an industry.

However, in Organizational behaviour, and in Organization's structuralism that holds the organization together, the individual rights are in one way subjected to Power Politics which exacts from a Leader, in terms of the styles of Leadership that he follows and in terms of the Vision that is imparted upon him.

Equality of Opportunity: Industrial Relations and the processes and procedures which it has, overall has clear cut aim to achieve equality of opportunity within an industry that a worker is employed within a workplace.

The Organization then champions campaigning efforts in such a case for those workers providing them equal treatment and opportunity in workplace free from preferences, prejudices, and artificial barriers quite often found otherwise in the workplace.

Living Wage: The process and procedures in Industrial Relations ensure that every employed individual, whether labourer or worker in one country makes a living wage. It goes without saying, the concerns that every humanitarian in our society has towards wage crisis and the consequences that follow, from that.

From a living wage, everybody benefits, be it workers, labourers, skilled, unskilled, and the poor. Living wage ensures everybody who works has money to spend, if when ploughed back into the society, improves economy, reduces inflation, and improves the common standard living conditions of the people.

Work Life Balance: Industrial Relations provide a common work-life balance to individuals and is extremely important so that it keeps them in a higher standard. It also helps one to enjoy the job to the maximum extent and so specifically creates a balance between highly productive environments as well as restricts them not to be excessively jubilant and aims for overall development of individuals.

16

Changing Needs Fulfilment of Human Needs

There are fundamentally two theories when one talks about Human Needs Theories and are Conservation Personalist Theories and Liberal Situationist (of type Situation-al) Theories.

Conservation Personalist Theories depict human beings as Creation Beings engaged in violent conflicts.

Liberal Situationist Theories provide conflicts due to human behaviour that normally gets resolved with ground for optimism.

Basic Human Needs

John Burton was the author of Deviance, Terrorism, and War and according to him people resolve destructive conflicts according to an expression given out by him.

Another theorist, Paul Sites in whose control Basis of Social Order, called in for eight essential needs whose satisfaction was required for Non-Deviant, Non-Violent and its individual behaviour.

According to him, this included, Primary Needs for Response, Stimulation, Security, and Recognition under Expression: RSSR and, Derivative Needs for Justice meaning Rationality and Control under Expression: J.

The importance of Maslow's Conception-al Human Development as Sequential Satisfaction of Basic Needs, grouped under Physiological, Safety, Love, Esteem, and Self Actualization cannot be forgotten.

For Burton, human needs offered a possible method of grounding fields of Conflict Analysis and Resolution resulted in a defensible theory of person.

Together with writers, Galtung, Coate, and Rosati, Burton provided new field of post-war social sciences which is Mechanistic, Utilitarianism, Behaviourism, Cultural relativism, and Hobbesian Realism.

In Burton's view, need for understanding destructive social conflicts are identity, recognition, security, and personal development.

Since State systems did not recognise identity, it gave way to modern ethno-nationalistic struggles as in the case of Palestinian-Israel Conflicts.

Human Needs Theory according to Burton's view has a relative object bias and gets across local, political, and cultural differences for understanding the source of conflict and ends up in designing conflict resolution process and founding conflict analysis and resolution as an autonomous discipline.

Conflict Theorists recognize this, no matter whether they agree with Burton or not.

Need for Human Needs Theories
Even after 1970s, there was persistence of irrational social struggles with its missing opportunities for their resolution.

However, this was explained based on theories Conservative Personal-ism and Liberal Situation-al-ism.

Conservative Personal-ism only aggravated situations that prompted human beings as creative beings driven to engage in violent conflicts. In this context sin, aggression and domination cannot be ruled out where non-violent, self-enforcing conflict resolution was considered a Utopian fantasy.

Liberal Situation-al-ism Theory provided Conflict Resolution providing ground for optimism.

This was by considering Environment and making adjustments to Environment surrounding the Black Box, which is considered as Metaphoric.

By this theory, given a certain environment or situation, people behave in a certain way around the Black Box in the given environment.

Here the following theories were studied based on a Black Box Premises.

Frustration typified Aggression by Pollard showed aggressive instincts wherever there was a goal-oriented activity.

Social Learning Theory considered humans as cognitive creatures whose ideas were shaped by social conditioning.

Post Freudian Psycho-Analytic Theory moved analogously away from primacy of families or cultural situations.

In all these Black Box Interactions, Burton saw an underlying similarity where Burton founds out that, Personalist (Social Learning) opened the door to limited social engineering by suggesting aggressive behaviours that can be environmentally controlled (as controls wielded on the Black Box).

Situation-al-ism Practitioners (Psycho Analytic Theory) found themselves unable or unwilling to reconstruct social environments, that is, moving away from families or cultural situations to the extend eliminating anti-social behaviours.

However, all the three theories when faced with a case of destructible violence, both the schools of thought (Personal-ism and Situational-ism) tended to respond as if objectionable behaviours could be modified by the right combination of Threats and Rewards.

Conservative Personalist when took the side of Deterrence, Liberal Situation-a-list went along with Positive Reinforcement or Pleasure.

That is curves of Pain and Pleasure will produce Consensual Behaviour.

Force need only be used according to both the theorists as a last resort.

It was also seen that both the theorists joined hands on a Political Realism or Realm and hence are Realists.

Realism

In Foreign Affairs, Realists emphasized relentless pursuit of power and power-based negotiations as the only alternative to inter group violence (Morgen than 1985).

In domestic affairs, they emphasized normative consensus and violent suppression of crimes (Cosier/Wilson – 1964/68).

However, Burton notices that none of these methods used by Realists did subscribe Transnational and Domestic Social Conflicts.

Realism hence was not Realistic.

It could not stop Ethno-Nationalistic wars, civil wars, violent struggles; manipulative coercion in a way making coercion was the prime focus in all their actions.

Burton then was of the opinion that Basic Human Needs Theory is the call of the hour that would challenge both Branches of Realism and would resolve the conflict by adopting the method of Optimistic Personal-ism in place of Conservative Personal-ism.

Basic Human Needs Theory

From these perspectives, three virtues of this theory seem notable.

The first one deals with Conflict resolvers and is asked to make a distinction of the numerous struggles that dealt with the Trinity of Force, Law, and Power based Negotiations.

The Second one is Equipped with Needs based Map of the field; Conflict Resolvers and Analyst understand the contradictions in Negotiations and Dispute Resolutions.

It was also encouraged to design the Resolution Process in such a way that it is around the Conflict's underlying Generic Issues.

In the third one, it was to be understood that Needs Based Approach and Destructive Social Conflicts were caused by a few manipulative leaders or is caused by the existence of Cultural or ideological differences.

Moreover, the Theory linked Conflict Analysis and Conflict Resolution as in the case of Huntington's Clash of Civilization Theory.

Limitations of Needs Theory

Objective bias for Socially and Politically salient needs in Human biology or nature is Essentialist, de-contextualized, and Historical.

John Burton's Counter (Arguments)

Transcending differences in class and gender are culturally driven.

Separation between Needs and Satisfiers, in terms of concepts like Identity and Security does not independently exist but exists out of Satisfiers.

If satisfiers are culturally bound, so are needs.

Major Role in Needs Fulfilment

Here it is known and bring it to notice a lack of theories of satisfiers when in equivalence theories of basic human needs (Mitchell).

That means one does not have as many theories of satisfiers as there are theories of basic human needs (Courtesy: Burton).

In the case while exploring an identity-based conflict, the need for identity is everywhere where-as what will satisfy the identity (Satisfiers) depends upon local history and changing circumstances.

Having known this, the needs management is required to take decisions as to how these needs can be fulfilled, no matter where there exist more satisfying needs or where there exist satisfiers.

It is also imperative to take a first-hand look at the reasons or causes for a lack of theory of satisfiers and is hereby determined as follows.

Lack of Satisfiers or Theory of Satisfiers exists because of existence of a Solution providing basic human needs and relativizing or marginalizing satisfiers.

It also exists because in Identity Based Conflicts, need for identity is everywhere but what satisfies it is present only if there is some local history behind it or there are changing circumstances that support it.

It is also well known that it is practically impossible to predict terminators of Identity based conflicts.

The occasion may also be used to introspect with some clear objectives on Identity based Conflicts as in the case of Middle East Conflicts.

Identity based Conflict or the Middle East Conflicts were based on Natural identities in question that were conceived in Religions and in Secular terms; Middle East Conflicts also exemplifies fact that in disregarding Burton's advocacy of conflict prevention, Needs Theory is generally applied after violent social conflicts erupted or happened and as a matter of fact it becomes difficult for making analysis of needs and satisfiers.

Needs Theory Development

The development of Needs Theory span across Predictive Study of Minorities, distinctions drawn between Individual and Group Needs as well as the significance of its Psychological Origins.

Ted R Gurr's predictive study of Minorities, in the case of minorities in the Middle East Conflict shows that the minorities are at risk and shows Needs Theorists a possible way to enhance the usefulness of the Theory.

A Regional or Global survey on how security and identity needs are conceived is an absolute must which will increase the level of satisfiers and satisfaction.

Development of Needs and Satisfiers applicable to conflicts are not primarily Ethno-Nationalist in nature, but may form other means of Group Definitions.

That is to say, the Group definitions need not be Ethno-Nationalist but groups in that place may be defined.

In order to know more about roles of basic needs in conflict, a better understanding of its psychological origins and processes are required through which one can learn that Needs become conscious motivators of Collective Action.

17

How flat is the world that we live in?

Friedman had crystallized thoughts about bringing this flattening of the world to America and the rest of the world.

According to him, flat world is one where technology and collaborative economics have created a new playing field.

He says, it definitely will change our theories of economics, politics, and jobs. It will increase competition and requires not only new skill sets, but a much more self-reliant, creative, and innovative mind set, based on discoveries that is many times revealed by Friedman, himself.

One thing is sure, in this flattening concept of his world, there sure exists Conflicts and there is no easy way, one is going to go through with the different kinds, to rationalize it based on an argument that Interactionist way is in Industrial Relations and dysfunctional ones destroy, the task, relationship, and process conflicts, which was at the first place supposed to build organizational integrity and Organizational development.

Even though, many may have their distinctive opinion on these matters, most certainly the facts remain that, the relationship conflicts remain dysfunctional to the organization in its many different participative models whereas Task conflicts destroy a group's morale.

Introspecting it, contrary to what we are made to think, Task conflicts especially if one group can keep it low, generally boosts the morale of the group and gives way to increased brainstorming around ideas, stimulates discussion among its members and helps the groups to be more innovative.

This may also hint at an increasing take at Goal setting theories, besides its cognitive roots, which sets alright an individual's take on matters, if he sets his purposes meaningful and delivers the outcomes, in a much more, straight forward manner, in a flattening world as is proposed by Friedman.

The opponent in such a situation, despite his reservations on this theory, may take Reinforcement under his glove and may argue for conditioning behaviour since reinforcement always conditions behaviour, a fact again, which is dealt well in Organizational dynamics.

18

Intellectual Capital Migration based on Behavioural Reforms

Since there is a wider gap that is imparted by Labour Relations, the combined effects call in for a bird's eye-view on Intellectual Capital Migration with its root in Behavioural Reforms advocated in Organizational Behaviour.

In this section, we touch briefly in identifying, studying, and defining the swaying influence and undue learning bias in Bureaucratic Decision Making and quantify the Amount of Behavioural Reforms in Incrementalism (Charles Lindblom in Muddling Through) in the light of an increasing bias seen in past policy making in all its six Emphases, which are Elite, Group, System, Institution, and organized Anarchy.

This may in-turn attempt a complete overhaul of the Existing or Frail Immigration System by introduction of an Intellectual Approach (Non-Political approaches of Luther Gulick in Classic Analysts) for Intellectual Capital Policy Migration in Public Policy Administration.

Bias amongst Bureaucrats

After amendments of the Hatch Act in 1993, public employees or federal employees were allowed to participate in election campaigns for electing the President, the Senate, and the Houses of Representatives.

Hence these attempts give way to non-bipartisan ideals of the public servant, that stood in the way of a politically polarized federal system, despite the call from Public Labour Unions to repeal acts like the Hatch.

On the other hand, the public servants, who worked in specialized departments like the Immigration and Naturalization saw the line of command from the President down through his Department Heads to every Federal Employee weaken despite existence of Recommendations from the Hoover Commission which introduced a Senior Civil Service in North America.

Intellectual Capital Migration

Introspection of the details of Intellectual Capital Migration, the Immigration & Naturalization Department is seen to destroy the Covenanted Civil Servant of the Companies Act 1793, which lays down that only Covenanted Civil Servants alone could be appointed to Civil posts anywhere in the world.

Further in capitalizing the trade, that have gone behind swapping Intellectual Capital from the Common Wealth Countries, the WAC Receipts (Cost of Intellectual Capital) were seen to have been given to Administration Officials (Workers) increasing the chances of exploitation of them by the Federal Agencies of what may otherwise have been a gradual progression of a civil servant becoming a Writer, a Factor, a Junior Merchant, and a Senior Merchant.

This is also seen to have increased the likelihood of inductive probabilistic approach which emphasis a shift in the objectives in addition to Environment (Reverse Migration), Circumstances that may lead to Reverse Migration, etc.

Hence to counter insurgency in the Public Servant Populace, instrumentality should be at +1.00, where a high performance based on a merit pay as well as adherence to iron quadrilaterals have to be made transparent to reduce the influence wielded by a particular special interest group on the remaining executives and sub-committees.

That is to say, all around the public domains in North America, Constitutionality of Acts like the Immigration Acts should be questioned.

On one side of the coin, the definitions of an Alien should be questioned and on the other side, the Permanence settlements of Aliens in North America should be questioned.

On account of such activities, many a times, this may call in for a Judicial Review on the said Demographic in North America and of the distinct ways of living adhered to by these Administrators in the North American counties of the Thirteen colonies, who are in fact Intellectual Group from Common Wealth countries, migrated to attain a promised set of ideals and be part of the promised land of the New World Order.

19

Minnowbrook Conferences

For reference, Minnowbrook Conference is held once in 20 years, starting from 1968. It brings together eminent scholars in Public Administration to reflect upon the latest innovations and inventions in the field of Public Administration.

The first Minnowbrook Conference as explained, brought out New Public Administration and the findings were combined with the names in a Report by Frank Marini in 1971 and was chiefly Anti-government in nature.

The Minnowbrook Conference - II brought out New Public Management and supported US Public Administration. It also brought out concepts around LPG (Liberalization, Privatisation and Globalization) and was held under the chairmanship of H George Frederickson.

The latest Minnowbrook Conference – Minnowbrook Conference-III was held in the year 2008 and addressed concerns around Global Terrorism, Economy, and Ecological Imbalance. Its focus was on structural and functional reforms and chiefly worked on the Concept of 3Es – Economy, Efficiency and Effectiveness. It was chaired by Rosemary O' Leary.

What lies ahead in the Minnowbrook Conferences (2028)?
Social Equity and fairness in Public Services

George Frederickson though took a long time about 40 years to write a book on Social Equity and Public Administration, is considered to have not taken a long time at all, when in comparison to the successive intervals of time that passes between consecutive Minnowbrook happenings.

Mr. Frederickson was instrumental in coining the term HRO or high reliability organization and was the chief person who coordinated the second Minnowbrook conference in the year 1988.

He also was a spiritual follower of Confucianism and in disguise an ardent follower of that faith which he believed gave a moral justification to Bureaucracy in populist countries.

His debates were circles around Rule of Man versus Rule of Law, methodologies around Good Official characters, concerns around Moral conventions and Governance and to remain in Meritocracy as a new order of Society.

Agreed, he also placed social equity as a third pillar in Public Administration alongside Efficiency and Economy.

But here there is an opportunity that may pose in the next Minnowbrook Conference, which is Mr. Frederickson's Social Equity as it relates to fairness of an organization and being fair in public service.

Fareness (a state of being fare) in equity franchise or being fair in public service was another question that ought to be answered as to where the governance framework should take everybody and the social equity that remains to be adjusted.

Since several references are seen to cause a disturbing outlook on the means of being fair to all concerned, may be his references to Black's Law of Dictionary should be equally subjected to a detailed discussion or a debate in the upcoming Minnowbrook Conferences.

Guerrilla Government of the 1970 in USA

According to Don Kettl Guerrilla Government happens all the time in the world of Public Budgeting and Finance.

Thanks to Rosemary O Leary in having brought the term Guerrilla Government to the normal household, many these days must talk about them in the day-to-day affairs and in chance encounters with their immediate pals.

In her narrative, The Ethics of Dissent: Managing Guerrilla Government, most of the issues at stake for a lovely public debate in the upcoming Minnowbrook Conference may arise from an incident that took place in Indiana, an off-road vehicle problem in a motorcycle event, code named Buffalo 100, named after John Buffalo who purchased 20 acres of land in the middle of the Hoosier National Forest in Indiana.

It seems after purchasing the parcel, Buffalo without notifying the Forest Guarding authority, a ranger by the name of Ferguson (who later was seen as a representative of Izaak Walton League of America Endowment), where Buffalo and his pals marked a 100-mile biking trail around and through the forest and let the motorized bikes do the damage, what damage, the trail might have led a clearing and a path to the explored and a clearing only to explore the wilderness of the forest land.

Anyway, Ferguson was unhappy in the year 1970 and decided to follow through instead of raising action, he decided to publish papers on the ORV (Off Road Vehicle) challenge facing National Parks notably in two conferences, one in 24th Great Lakes Park Training Institute and subsequently in February 1970 in the 20th Annual Great Lakes District Conference.

What he conveyed there had done enough damage to the institution of biker trail made by ORV users in the Hoosier National Forest and in theory he agreed with Dr. Diana Dunn the then Director for National Recreation and Park Association that it was intolerable for the forest supervisor to manage eco-catastrophes involving bikes and not that much the Forest vehicles that were supposed to have made an entry in a few occasions through the clearing made by the bikers or the ORVs.

So, this in turn turned the argument in favour of the Buffalo and his pals who were now allowed to use their vehicles in a small but approved areas around the forest.

In 1971 the Indiana General Assembly wanted a bigger piece of the parcel and started enacting legislation on mandatory registration of off-road vehicles that used the Buffalo trail.

In particular was the disapproval of Earl Wilson who could not but accept the ORV motorcade or cavalcade without his permission that prompted the regional forester close the facility with immediate action. So HNF would not host any ORV adventures.

It did not stop there then.

In 1972 the President Richard Nixon issued an executive order to control the use of ORVs to ply on these clearing which was the sole contribution of the supposedly pioneer Buffalo or his so-called proclaimed acts.

Now the order protects resources of the land, and promotes safely of all users of land in bikes, ORVs, or Forest vehicles and what-not; and minimizes conflicts among various users of the land.

The explorers of the land here Buffalo and his pals are in other words questioned for the veracity shown by him and the public governance here is sped up to grant discourse and control for maximizing governmental interventions and duplicity in getting the parcels into a pseudo governmental property, in instituting duplicity in erecting establishments thereby transforming forest land and the proprietary parcels that surround the forest to establishments instituted by the sole discriminants of government bureaucracy rightfully termed by Leory as Guerrilla Government.

So as far as the definitions go, Guerrilla Government is the intermittent interventions by government executives negating the rights of parcel owners and the farming community to the making of future governmental establishments on private holdings based on a quasi-governmental order.

To say the least, this is one of the most formidable topics in exercising caution to the use of degenerative Guerrilla Government tactics of Government executives in exploiting the parcels and getting them converted to business outfits and establishments, all controlled by a semi executive order.

Ferguson might have sued the Forest authorities later due to ethical reasons from within but the real question to be asked is how many Fergusons it might take to speed up dissecting proprietary parcels near the forest land to erect in its place, governmental establishments and machinery instituted by Guerrilla Government and their kingpins, thereby making private ownership and proprietary parcels a near impossibility or a gambling exercise in Law for the surviving (North) American franchise.

20

Agitations to win Social Security Benefits from USG (the US Government)

Thomas Jefferson has quoted as saying "I'm a great believer in luck and I find the harder I work, the more I have of it".

So, Today I would like to talk about Retirement Benefits, those benefits that are so dear to us in India for hi-tech workers like us where we have our Provident Fund and in some foreign countries, for NRIs, those benefits come under the umbrella 401(k) Benefits and Social Security Benefits, etc.

We know it is a straightforward thing, while you are working in a concern, by law, you have to pay a portion of your income for retirement benefits which is mandatory in most of the countries including India.

The rate at which you pay for Social Security contributions is reflected off at a minimum rate in some countries like USA, it should be a minimum of 6.25% and then your employer matches that, so ultimately you get the Social Security benefits around 12.4% of your own compensation or the employee compensation.

But there is a quirk or twist in the way Social Security Compensations are treated in the USA.

By Law, all the employee whether you work on a work visa or Green Card, or a US Citizen is bound to make a contribution to Social Security Benefits but only a Green Card or US Citizen is eligible to avail the Social Security Benefits.

This means a majority of the NRIs who did not become a Green Card or US Citizen is at a disadvantage since they may have already made the Social Security Contribution but unable to avail the Social Security benefits in USA and for the ones who have gone back to India after serving a considerable number of years in USA, are still unable to avail the US Social Security Benefits.

Working in the USA during the first decade of the year 2000, we felt this was not the right way to disburse one's Social Security Earnings in the USA especially for Indian citizens who were on a work visa in USA or who were Green Card holders in USA but now settled in India.

And hence, in our stay in USA, we agitated against the US Government in peaceful means by carrying placards and walked around the streets in Washington DC, in New Jersey, wherever we could, we are only a handful of people and often times not troubled by the political establishments there.

Like us, many Indian citizens might have agitated so that they could avail the US Social Security Benefits even after getting settled in India after their service in the USA and all our hard work finally seemed to have started to pay off because this subject or point was making some headlines in both India and the USA.

On 9th March 2016, Sushma Swaraj, the then Minister for External Affairs in a statement that was laid on the table of the Lok Sabha, informed the House that India has signed SSA or the Social Security Agreement (SSA) or Totalization Agreements with 18 different countries to protect Indian Professionals and skilled workers working abroad and provided benefits to them.

Exportability was the main benefit which was brought in as part of the Social Security Agreement or Totalization Agreement, where an SSA that is signed between India and a foreign country enabled the Indian Worker who was employed in that foreign country to remit his accumulated social security contribution made in that foreign country to India in the event the Indian worker relocated to India after his work and service in that foreign country.

The benefits which were listed in the Social Security Agreement also included the Indian citizen not to make double social security contributions, if he was already making a social security contribution in India based on the sum or amount provided to him by way of Employee contributions.

It was also told to us that India was working on a Social Security Agreement or Totalization Agreement with the USA and the hope is that we will be successful in executing that agreement soon.

To get an idea of the size of total funds that the USA alone has to pay to the wage earners who were NRIs in USA for the service time they spend in the USA is quite high and may easily run upward of six billion dollars plus interest if you consider the past 25 to 30 years of Indian immigration to the US alone.

So, let's hope the discussions for SSA go on between India and US and hopefully something better emerges in the future.

21

Land Administration of Privately owned Parcels and Monument Assets

This is a short article on Land Administration of privately owned Parcels and Monument Assets in the Indian subcontinent.

To locate the origin of parcels, historically in the Indian Princely States (both British and Native kings), some parcels and monument assets are heritage and parcel, whereas in British North America after the Declaration of Independence in 1777 which formed the United States, parcels owned in North America by the British people in the newly formed United States then, might have after prolonged revisions considered nocturnal and screwed up.

Monument reclamation has resulted in monumental losses for private land holders, especially when done by the public in the name (guise) of deceased and eminent personals who themselves were private landholders who had left nothing but a lasting impression on the lives of their people in India.

Before the independence of India, though India was ruled by the British, it was also home to Rajas and their strong, powerful, equivocal princely states. Apart from the larger dominion, that was ruled by the British that was British India, several small princely states existed, some of which were British Princely States and some of them princely states ruled by eminent and powerful (native) kings.

When one considers inhabitable land from when on in the Indian sub-continent, land was earmarked by scores of legendary historical figures and as such the source of its denominations is not similar in Indian states, let alone not similar within an Indian state due to the complexity of its formation and of its historical roots of its formation.

However, it is without fail that the authenticity of such documentation exist in different forms within a state for certainly earmarked regions, depending upon where the source of such documents be traced, depends upon where the Land & Buildings belonged in which era under whose governance where it was put in agreement or be assigned in which form under whose rule it remained in existence where the rulers themselves without being questioned or defeated and under which act it was formalized until what time until all of its formations were dissolved from the Indian Raj (Raja era) to its democratic rules and acts formed under the present Indian dominion and subsequently in the Indian States (since State subject) in the greater country of India.

For illustration purposes, let us consider,

- the origination of Land Records in the State of Kerala, and
- On Land Administration that were done in Andra State after its formation in the year 1953, in particular in the NTR Era (Shri N T Ramarao), to get some basic hints on land administration that was done in British Provinces, British or otherwise Princely States, Indian Union and in the days after the Indian State Reorganization Act in the year 1957.

Land Administration in some parts of India

Illustrations from Kerala – Origination of Land Records

Kerala is believed to be land given to Brahmins by Parashurama, who according to some historians, those Brahmins and their dependents were people who have migrated from North India after Parishit Tampuran (King Parishit) whose dynastical destruction brought about by a Serpent, drove away all the

Serpent worshipping people from North India who all had innate knowledge in Agriculture, Vastu, Trade, … and settled down in areas that spanned from Coastal Gokarna in Karnataka to Kanyakumari in Tamil Nadu where every Keralite who inhabits it now is considered equal to each other with all of them having certainly Brahminical roots which are unique in their existence, their way of life and culture embedded in their common Shudra roots (some argue all men in Kerala born Shudra with practice get elevated to their Brahminical existence); most certainly all men in Kerala are considered equal from mythology times, with references from King Mahabali's times onwards.

Kerala is chiefly Travancore, Kochi, and princely states of British India (Kannanur and Kozhikode) and parts of the Madras Province (Malabar district and Kasaragod which itself was part of South Canara district), where there was never an acquisition of land in any of its territorial domain after 1934 by means of a war or a calamity.

Hence, each of the land assignments are treated appropriately in each of its earmarked locations and the historical roots of lineage and legacy, preserved and maintained by the present-day Indian state governments so that it keeps proper historical reference in terms of documentation which is of utmost importance to distinguish first class land given by the King to his people in the pre-Indian independence era.

This is to be treated differently from government land given to a certain section of people in independent India or encroachments in the government land in independent India that has emerged much later after 1947 in Dominion of India and in British Princely states (Cannanore and Calicut) and after 1957 in the integrated state of Thiru-kochi (after 1957 majority of it was Kerala).

In Travancore, origination of land records was based on land given by the King of Travancore to his people in three classes, namely, Brahmaswam (Land given to Kerala Brahmin class people), Devaswom (Land given to Temple and Temple Administration) and Pandara-vaka-Pattom (Land given to normal populace) along with sales deed to Private Land Holdings for various purposes, mainly, for Agriculture, Vocational Leadership shown in select trade, profession, Honorary titles in trade (Anthraperu), Celibacy, Karam Ozhivu, and many other categories.

In Kochi however, revenue collection was done by the Thampuran before 1957 by giving due powers to Paliath who were the sole authorities for revenue collection in the State of Kochi.

Land Administration Reforms in Andra after 1953 – Revenue Administration

During British rule in India (whole of British India), revenue districts were made under Taluk which served as the basis for basic units in Revenue Administration; however, blocks and their headquarters as development units were brought in much later to the Andra State probably in the late 1950s and during early 1960s.

In rural areas in Andra, they were co-terminus (Reference: Advice & Dissent, YV Reddy).

It is worthy to note, read, and learn on the reformation of district administration in Andra, mostly in the NTR Era (Shri N T Ramarao) who wanted to split each Taluk or block into three or four units bringing the rural administration close to the people of Andra. NTR was chiefly successful in taking the Area Approach for the reorganization of Taluks and Blocks into Mandals, both Revenue Mandals and Developmental Mandals, where the rural government was co-terminus with the Developmental Mandals.

Also, during his tenure, the post of Village Officers was made redundant and government officers were appointed as full-time staff to carry on their duties in the villages.

Along with all the reformations that was brought about by NTR, what went into oblivion were the age-old Patwari system in Andra villages from the British times which relied on Patwari or Karnam to maintain revenue records along with Village Munsif, optionally called Patels in some areas tasked with Revenue Collections were Mali Patel and Police Administration matters in rural areas were called Police Patel.

Recent Wakf Claims and Developments in the State of Karnataka

Recently a lot of hue and cry is over the Wakf claims made by the Wakf board on land now being owned by the regular populace in India of what it was previously being surrendered to the Wakf board by the then Muslim owners of the land a few generations ago despite the same Muslim owners or their successors went ahead with selling them to Communities that may be Muslim or Non-Muslim.

In a similar manner, Wakf also has made claim to a lot of monumental assets that are monuments themselves (historically important mosques) that span across Karnataka where most of it currently State property, but Wakf claims that it is their property in other words the Wakf claim on it goes on.

By Law, the common franchise is kept guessing on the Wakf matter since the Wakf board themselves have rules and law quite distinct and outside the Indian Penal system but considered legal for Muslims in the Secular Republic of India.

Many buyers of land who went ahead to purchase land under Wakf claim without knowing this fact, now have to battle with the Wakf claim, mainly because they were not informed of that in fact even the Banking system in India were blamed not to have taken note of this fact, while performing collateral checks, fact being the existence of Wakf board and their claims on their ever-expanding land and legal basis in India were not known to the Banking system while providing home loans to new homeowners in these Wakf claimed lands.

Many argue that the Wakf board need not be consulted, nor their opinion taken in face value on matters concerning these Wakf claimed properties because in all the Wakf board there is no diverse representation of people (since Wakf is represented only by Muslim people alone), even when the land claimed by Wakf were believed to be once ceded by their Muslim owners in the past few generations to the Wakf board themselves.

Matter of fact is the timing of the issue and on the control seeking of when the Wakf board and law got the General acceptance in the Indian legal parlance and on when these lands were ceded to the Wakf board by the Muslim land owners a few generations ago and whether the acceptance of the Wakf board and its law is made effective in the Indian legal system by predating of its existence from thence on, remains to be seen.

22

Reading The Travancore State Manual...

(Reading The Travancore State Manual, keeping aside the reaffirmed self-assertions or self- citations for the benefit of the Princely State as a whole even when The Travancore State Manual is blamed to have deviated from the true history of Kerala and the history of its people, agreeing completely the need for British India shadow rulings on Indian Princely states in Kerala in pre-independent India, a definite need during those times of impending wars and an unstable world order.)

Recently I went through the Travancore State Manual, believed to be written by V Nagam Aiyah in 1906 who was Dewan Peishcar, Travancore during the 1900s. I did not do a detailed reading but from going through the section on History of Colonization of Kerala by Kerala Brahmins, I felt The Travancore State Manual gave a completely different view of Kerala History than what was given in Keralolpathi, written by Shri Shankunni Menon.

Few facts I will try to list from Keralolpathi first and later I will condense my observations on The Travancore State Manual.

Reading through Keralolpathi...

According to Keralolpathi, Kerala was land given to (Kerala) Brahmins by Lord Parashurama that extended from coastal Gokarna in Karnataka to Kanyakumari in Tamil Nadu.

Not all Brahmins but only those Brahmins (Kerala Brahmins) who were serpent worshippers from North India were driven out because a serpent did kill Parishit Tampuran (King Parishit) (Pandava's lineage) despite his best efforts to save himself from serpents were futile, as is cited in the book.

According to Keralolpathi, Kshatriyas were not killed by Parashurama but became Nairs who assumed the Sudra Class and willingly gave up the sacred thread and accompanied Kerala Brahmins according to the directions given by Lord Parashurama. Again, these Nairs who wanted to go back to their Kshatriya roots did so after the performance of Hiranyagarbham (which was likewise performed by later Samoothiris of Malabar as well as later Travancore kings) which is a ritual believed to be done under the directions of Lord Parashurama himself where those Nairs who participated in Hiranyagarbham can wear the sacred thread and can become Kshatriyas. (Remember, Lord Parashurama is a Chiranjeevi or is an immortal person).

Reading through The Travancore State Manual...

As far as The Travancore State Manual goes, even though there were a lot of details given about Travancore and its history in the year 1906, most of its history as depicted in The Travancore Manual is way different than what is given in Keralolpathi, the point to be noted is, who or under whose direction it is written and why it is written differently is a subject of countless debates, the majority may say it is different because the British or the (English) rulers in pre independent India during that time wanted it written that way so that the Princely state withstood a lot of destabilizing attempts made on the State given the normal populace took most of the burden in mending social structures around each communities in deriving proper conventions and procedures (a fact even today in for the historical state of Kerala in Independent India) despite the presence of agonized truths and faltering pride for each and every members of the so called surviving communities in Kerala.

It is definitely debatable or may be just the truth which shows even today how improvised we remain as political and apolitical entities to have mend in a sort of way so that we made sure the waves of freedom be there for everybody in our State even when the State breathes in and out all the procedures and conventions, the ones that were written under the directions of Britain during the difficult times of World Wars (20th Century) and during the most unfavourable world order of the early 20th century.

It also shows how much exploited Keralites as one people would have been if we did not have strong native rulers in all our Princely States in Kerala (pre independent India), who gave us the basics of infrastructure, development, and a unique cultural (Kerala) framework so that the State remained independent and working despite all the nuances that it had to bear throughout its existence.

Reading through The Travancore State Manual and its differences from Keralolpathi

Few observations in The Travancore State Manual; Nairs in The Travancore State Manual are pictured as Naga tribes living in forest land in Kerala where this is not true since Nairs have no relations to the Naga tribe from Nagaland. etc.

Also, Kshatriyas according to The Travancore State Manual were seen as Kings invited to rule Kerala from the East Coast of India, invited by none other than Lord Parashurama is also not true. Imagine Kshatriyas from the East coast have no relation to Kerala or its formation or its history, also why should Lord Parashurama invite Kshatriyas from the East Coast of India, the same Kshatriyas who were killed by Lord Parashurama according to the same book, The Travancore State Manual.

Again, according to The Travancore State Manual, Hiranyagarbha (Hiranyagarbham) is depicted as a ritual to bring back religious converts from caste Hindu back to the Hindu caste which is again ideally written with a reference to a Perumal king (King with a Chera or Pandya dynastical connection as was evident in references to the King of Cranganore or Kodungallur) who though was believed to have gotten converted to Islam, died later in Arabia, their successors back in Kerala were said to have performed Hiranyagarbham ritual to bring him back to caste Hindu according to The Travancore State Manual.

So, it is interesting to be reading The Travancore State Manual, where it makes you think about the value of historical information and to what minutest detail is depicted about Travancore, as it existed as a Princely State in the early 20th century.

23

Possession of land by a Primitive or Dispossessed state on the basis of Cultural Biases

Do you know the difference between Republic of Ireland, and Northern Ireland?

Now some history.

Gaelic Ireland emerged from 1st century AD.

From the 5th century Ireland was Christianised.

In the 8th century to 11th century Viking raids took place and early settlement in Ireland emerged, primarily with a lot of Catholic settlements.

Following the 12th century Anglo Norman invasion, England claimed sovereignty over Ireland.

After the Tudor conquest in the 17th century, which led to the colonisation of Ireland by the protestant settlers, it led to materially disadvantage the Catholic settlers.

This meant Catholic majority Ireland was made part of by Protestant settlers from England.

Wars emerged and in 1948 Ireland of Republic was a realty with a portion of Ireland with protestant majority becoming Northern Ireland part of United Kingdom.

So, to see Ireland, we have Republic of Ireland and Northern Ireland, where the Protestant majority folks live in Northern Ireland whereas the Catholic majority lives in Republic of Ireland.

Both the entities speak mostly Irish language but yet are divided into two states.

But what I try to convince you here is very briefly all arguments that may favour an Irish person from Republic of Ireland to possess land in Northern Ireland on the basis of a settler from a primitive or dispossessed state which in our case is Gaelic Ireland on the basis of cultural biases or cultural ties it has with both the Irelands, Northern Ireland and Republic of Ireland.

So, we discuss here the arguments that may favour an Irish settler from Republic of Ireland to possess land in Northern Ireland citing common leniency of being a Gaelic Ireland settler, generations ago.

So, what are the arguments that may favour such a person?

According to David Garrad, a writer, restricting ownership rights through a medium of foreign legislation may not override forms of restrictions, however the term cultural property may give some hope to the Gaelic Ireland settler who may enhance the so-called property rights which are in existence for a titular owner in terms of ownership on structures or monuments erected in Northern Ireland from a Gaelic period, etc.

Signifying a group's cultural assets may run in history, which may comprise of properties that these groups have which are distinct in terms of their ways of life, including, language, customs, institutions which the new entity who is the Victorian entity (Protestant England) owned based on a specific piece of regulation during the 1700s is both arguably common to both the Gaelic settlers as well as the Northern Irish settlers.

From the work, Dispossessed State by Sarah L Maurer, this particular assertion of the Rights of property was the opening shot in a campaign of violent resistances that drove the British state almost entirely out of Ireland, in particular from the places that made up Republic of Ireland.

This in turn made the Anglican Protestants who were conquerors or immigrants of a forcible sect now realize that their properties seemed to be disintegrating into a nothingness of infinite alienability in the places that made up Republic of Ireland whereas for the native ones from Ireland, including Gaelic Ireland, their properties were imagined as a right to a spatial zone whose prerogatives could not be extinguished by a mere state order in Northern Ireland.

Hence an Irish settler though from a different sect could still survive in Gaelic Ireland or both the Irelands put together whereas an English settler may not survive in places that made up Republic of Ireland.

So, think about it, especially the conquerors, the cultural property is an important factor that decides the ingenuity of a place be it after zillions of conquests that a place like Gaelic Ireland is subjected to, may still realize their actual roots so that they accommodate or may still favour a Catholic Irish settler in Northern Ireland as opposed to an English settler in the Republic of Ireland.

24

Gestures and a thought to distinguish Drama from Oration

Sometimes it is like Gestures and Thought leave more than a thought for Dramatics to evolve beyond the Primitive Man habits.

To come to the point, ...

Language as per some linguists comes in two forms, Static and Dynamic.

The static part of the Language is Technical Linguistic with its own formations of it in terms of its structure, grammar, words, etc. According to the static form, Language is an object and not a process.

The dynamic part of the Language is Language Imagery, and it combines Gestures with the static structure of the language be it, grammar, words, etc. According to the dynamic form of language, language is a process and not an object.

Now this is a good time to think about what evolved first in a Language.

Is it its dynamic form or its static form?

We know the Neanderthal or Primitive Man communicated using sign languages and gestures played a big part in the evolution of languages. When it is fully developed, we have a static form of language, which is apt with the correct formations, be it describing context or in expressing fully formed sentences with or without an imagery.

What will now happen if you combine Static and Dynamic forms of a Language?

That definitely results in a Dialectic which is a form of Language, where the static form is well developed, and Dynamic form expressed in terms of a unit called Growth Point which is a unit of Dialectic where imagery and linguistic contents are combined.

Here also the unstable element is - Dynamic and what goes stable is - Static Element until a Stop Order happens which is when the Speaker legibly conveys information in terms of language structure, very indicative of a Static Form.

Now what is speech and what is dramatics?

Some say the Kerala artform Ottamthullal is based on pure Speech or is rendered as a static form of its Language, Malayalam whereas the Kerala artform Kathakali is pure Drama or is rendered as a dynamic form of its Language, Malayalam.

So, from our discussions, Speech is an object and not a process and is well formed more advanced than dramatics which is based on the dynamic form of language with gestures articulating and supplementing any language used.

Speech can very well survive without a lot of dynamic gestures embedded in them. The more dynamic gestures get embedded in speech, it turns dramatic or normal conversation attain a dramatic plateau.

Now how beneficial it is to include gestures in speech without making the conversations or proclamations or oration turn into drama is all left to the speaker to decide.

But before we let you go; one aspect should be clear in everybody's mind. And it is none other than the types of

Gestures that are commonly embedded in Speech and used to convey in strict language terms.

Gestures usually when combined in speech are in four forms, namely, Gesticulation, where there is presence of speech; Emblems where there is an optional presence of speech, Pantomime where there is an obligatory absence of speech and Sign Language where there is a complete absence of speech.

From a linguistic properties' standpoint, Gesticulation and Emblems have no linguistic properties whereas Pantomime and Sign Language has a lot of Linguistic properties.

Now the big question?

Do you acknowledge the presence of gestures in speech and if you do, to what extend you make it obvious by rendering a rather unclear message in sentences complemented by gestures which articulate them?

So, just think about it...

25

Rolling back on Free Trade

(How much benefited are we from Global Trade these days?)

Despite agreeing on nothing economically, there is an apolitical consensus that is emerging in the Western world, especially in the US, to roll back on Free Trade, policy wise a complete reversal is what US did from their previous stand.

Looks like the developed western world is indeed moving away in a big way from the concept of Globalization. Marked as the Globalization Backlash by Raghuram G Rajan and Rohit Lamba, what is to be blamed is the rising conflicts between United States and China for geo-political supremacy, that is causing all the havoc.

Now does this present itself an opportunity for India is to be answered as we progress along.

In case at the paramount of this conflict between Western powers and China, if they apply wide ranging sanctions against each other, western corporations fear that the Supply Chain that runs through China will be disrupted and productions may stall, since it is no secret that China is the largest supplier of goods and services to the world.

Also, some natural and unnatural events or activities have prompted situations like the Covid outbreak in the past, when Chinese production was disrupted and many in the West thought it presented an opportunity to diversify production, in terms of a strategy known as the China + 1 strategy.

What is this China + 1 strategy?

This is a western strategy where, for every segment of the supply chain that is in China, they look for an alternate producer in another country, that remains friendly to the Western countries.

Given the attractiveness of the domestic market, some global supply chains are said to be looking for India as their China + 1 producer.

But everything that glitters is not gold.

So, despite some decisions in that manner from some corners of the Corporates, India may not be the preferred destinations for such companies, primarily because the input tariffs are still higher in India for instance, the import duties for materials in the sense raw materials are higher, etc.

Let us say if that is addressed, then also there exists the physical distance between the western countries and India as a manufacturing hub and then there are other factors like Nearshoring and Reshoring.

Now, what is this Nearshoring and what is Reshoring?

Nearshoring or the gravity model of trade as it is called is a phenomenon where a good amount of business activity thrives within the purview of a continent, for instance 40% of the North American business thrives within the continent of North America, 50% of East Asian trade is within East Asia with China or Taiwan as the epicentre of trade related activities and 70% of European trade is well within Europe.

So, Nearshoring in the China + 1 strategy would always go in favour of let us say Mexico for North American business, Romania for European trade as well as Taiwan or China for the East Asian trade.

It does not stop there.

Some experts from the west say that instead of the China + 1 partner strategy or Nearshoring, that is instead of Nearshoring they think that reshoring is the right approach for them. What is reshoring? It is the concept where Supply Chain which is outsourced to a cheap labour-intensive place like China is brought back to the source country or countries in the western bloc.

Since the labour is expensive in the West, they feel a great worth or value for Automation whereby labour-intensive work could be automated in some foreign country and then Re-shored so that large sums of manufacturing processes could be saved in the long run as a result of this reshoring.

So, Nearshoring goes with the China + 1 partner strategy and Reshoring in a big way supports Automation in every manufacturing and production processes which is meant to get the Supply Chain back to the Western countries.

So, where does this leave countries like India in the bigger concept in the days after Globalization, in the new era of Nearshoring and Reshoring is entirely left to be seen.

Let us keep our hopes high! Ciao.

26

Banking risks in the Global Housing Market

It is at best contentious when and where the Asset prices depart from the fundamentals in particular in a non-housing boom market considering the fact that house prices are a function of the interest rate, household incomes, local demographics and local zoning regulations which itself mandate the volume of housing supply.

In the US at least, rising income inequality (Refer: Raghuram Rajan; Fault Lines) in other words initiated political pressure prompting measures that offer easy credit to the middle- or low-income groups, chiefly in the form of bank lending or bank loans for housing so that the middle- or low-income populace in the US may acquire households in a reasonable neighbourhood.

Since the real estate sector in the US boomed as a result of these actions, this in turn gives way to more in the job market and results in growing consumption, despite an inevitable postponement of the housing loan instalments of the housing loan taken by these US middle-low-income earners push them to a state of indeterminate future.

In other words, as a result of these actions, let us assume the American dream is realized for all sections of people momentarily in the USA.

In addition, whenever the Feds (Federal Reserve) decreases the interest rate, housing loans become affordable for the low- or middle-income groups in the US. But this in turn ends up in a booming real estate market driving the prices up and hence in order to control inflation, Feds again try to raise the interest rate.

This over a prolonged number of years may necessarily impede the capacity of the borrower in the low-and-middle income groups in the USA for loan payments, giving rise to an increase in bank's Non-Performing Assets (Bank loans) especially given the fact that banks themselves may have financed these long-term loan assets by borrowing in the short term from the financial markets.

Accumulation of bad assets in light of short-term finances especially from NBFC (Non-Banking Finance Companies) or MF (Mutual Fund) for banks facing an already frozen short term money market with a frenzied depositor run may in turn lead the banks in US to go bust as might have happened in the 2008 Lehman Brothers crises. Shortly after, in the UK, the Northern Rock debacle was no different a banking downfall or debacle more or less in the same year.

Indian scenario

In India also banks are exposed to different types of risks in particular Credit Risk in the Credit Portfolio from the perspective of banking regulation and governance (RBI) as well as Market rate risk in the Investment portfolio.

During 2003, the financial leadership in India came up with Investment Fluctuation Reserve and its main intention was to protect the Investment portfolio of the banks in India against Market risk beyond whatever protection was offered to them by the Basel Norms.

In addition to maintaining Capital Charge for Market Risks, measures taken by the RBI included provisioning for Standard Assets, provisioning was done by the RBI as a way to counter risks arising in the Credit Portfolio.

To surmise, these regulatory measures taken by the RBI, in the light of high credit growth in the real estate sector, credit card receivables, and loans qualifying as capital market exposure are seen to historically control situations where there exists a high loan default rate as a result of a volatile housing market.

27

History of Regulatory Measures used to manage bad loans in the Indian Banking Sector

(History of Measures taken by the RBI to recognize, track, and restructure bad loans (NPAs) in the Indian Banking Sector)

Bad Loans or NPA (Non-Performing Assets) are formed when the borrowers' default on loan payments, the default or non-payment of loan if it is more than 90 days, the loan will be Sub-standard, between 90 days till 180 days may remain Substandard and doubtful, and anything beyond 180 days is considered Loss Asset.

RBI being the central bank of India does fundamentally two jobs, one that of a regulator of banks and another crafting and overseeing the money market or overseeing the monetary policies of India.

As part of this, the measures taken by the RBI also involves recognizing a bad loan in a bank in India, track the bad loan and if possible, provide guidelines to restructure the loan so that it tends to remain a Standard Asset for the bank.

In other words, RBI helps banks to manage the NPA effectively so that in the long run banks tend to reduce their NPA (Non-Performing Assets) and convert them into Standard Assets, thereby increase the revenue from banks out of loan assets as well as make the loan product revenue generating from a banking business standpoint.

Certainly, and more appropriately taking a historical look at this loan management by the RBI, one can see a lot of financial and monetary measures taken by the RBI which has recognized bad loans in banks, helped track them as well as restructure them if there is a possibility existing.

As part of it, in this article, we tend to examine the timelines RBI as a monetary authority and regulator of banks, has come out with measures that helped manage the loan assets in banks in India where we try to depict it from when it started to the most recent of them all.

Timelines of the measures taken by RBI to curb bad loans (NPAs) in the banking sector

The times lines of RBI measures to monitor and restructure NPAs or bad loans of the banks it supervises are as given below.

Loan Modifications in USA by Federal Reserve (1929-39): Historically and conceptually, the concept of loan restructuring can be traced back to measures taken in the USA during the Great Depression, when loan modification was introduced for the first time. To prevent banks, foreclose the loan and auction the homes, a string of mortgage modifications schemes was devised in the USA for those loans which buyers were not able to service the debt. The main reason why it was done was to curtail homelessness and the economic impact which was spreading during the Great Depression period in the USA.

Rescheduling in India (1978): In India, first time loans were restructured in non-industrial accounts was in 1978, when RBI advised banks to reschedule loans taken by people affected by natural calamities and floods.

Health Code System (1980): In the mid-1980s management of NPAs were left to banks and their auditors where in the year 1985 a Health Code system was introduced by RBI which put the Non-Performing loans in 8 categories starting from 1 which was satisfactory to 8 which were indicative of bad loans.

IRAC (1990): In 1990, following the Narasimhan Committee, a structured framework was put in place with the introduction of Income Recognition and Classifications norms. Earlier it was meant for restructuring industrial accounts but its scope was extended in 2008 to cover non industrial accounts also.

Prudential Norms on Capital Adequacy (1992): Prudential norms on Capital Adequacy was introduced by the RBI in the year 1992. Basel Committee issued International Banking regulations and with the introduction of prudential norms, there was policy adherence with international regulations on Capital Adequacy. In India, this meant any loan account is an NPA if it was unpaid for 1 year in the year 1992 and this gradually reduced to half an year in 1995. In the year 2003-04 any loan which remained unpaid for 90 days was termed an NPA with the concept of introduction of the concept of past-dues which was loan unpaid for 30 days or more.

Forbearance and not Restructuring (2000): In the early days of 2000, the emphasis for loan default was to provide the borrowers with alternate tools such as increased repayment periods, forbearance in the form of evergreening of bank loans by taking the route of offer of additional loans, etc.

Corporate Debt Restructuring (2001): CDR was put in place in the year 2001 but it could not help the lenders or their agonies in the Indian context. When it was first envisaged, CDR was supposed to offer a timely transparent way of restructuring debts which were 20 crores of rupees or more, outside the ambit of DRT (Debt Recovery Tribunal) or BIFR (Board for Industrial and Financial Reconstruction). RBI also directed the banks to consider any substandard asset that was restructured be a standard asset if it was properly backed by securities and remained in good standing. In other words, any sub-standard asset that was referred to the CDR platform was guaranteed not to be downgraded with a chance to become a standard asset with proper backing of securities.

Review (2001): In 2001, there was a review in place by following the best practices from BIS (Bank of International Settlements) and FASB (US Financial Account Standards Board).

There were revisions on how principal based restructuring was done as well interest restructuring was brought to light.

Restructuring on a standard account was done where standard classification was retained if instalment of principal alone was rescheduled and the loan fully secured. Rescheduling of interest on the other hand entailed amount of sacrifice measured in present value terms that must be written off or provided for. Same rules for substandard loan, substandard classification was retained after restructuring on it was done.

Rescheduled substandard account was also upgraded to standard account only after an year of satisfactory performance in terms of payment of interest or principal.

Also, DCCO (Date of commencement of commercial operation) in a project played a key role in deciding upon the subject: Classification of loans.

Credit Information System (2007): RBI tried in the years 2007 and 2008 to set up a Credit Information System where the idea was that banks share data regarding their share of bad loans. But due to untimely updates of data by sometimes only the Lead Bank in a Consortium Agreement, this scheme did not bring in the intended result as the CIS was originally planned or set to achieve.

Measures not implemented (2011): RBI advice on providing for provisioning for restructured loan at 5% and directions such as once a loan is restructured, loan is substandard/bad were not implemented due to stiff opposition from the banking communities.

SDR (2013): SDR or Strategic Debt Restructuring was where under RBI's guidance, banks convert a firm's debt into bank's equity with ownership rights in the firm. Banks convert part of their debt in stressed companies to equity resulting all the time in Management changes in stressed companies.

Idea was to force borrowers to bear the first loss and not lenders and force promoters to be bold during such scenarios. During the same year, when SDR was instrumental, RBI supervision changed from CAMELS to RBS; CAMELS being Capital adequacy, Asset Quality Management, Management, Earnings, Liquidity and Systems Control to Risk Based Supervision.

CRILC (2014): CRILC was Central Repository of Information on Large Credits, a reporting system that was run and maintained by the Reserve Bank of India and it was where banks reported data regarding their share of bad loans which are 5 crores or above. Data was reported through this system managed by RBI where banks reported all accounts turning bad on a weekly basis and all standard loans were reported on a monthly basis.

AQR – Asset Quality Review (2015): AQR process was also an initiative set by RBI where AQR was a team effort in recognizing bad loans where the identification of bad loans in banks ran for three months with the clean-up processes starting in the fourth month in an year. Any bad assets of banks with a potential to harm the depositor trust were identified and reported under the AQR scheme.

S4A Scheme (2016): S4A or the Scheme for Sustainable structuring of Stressed Assets followed SDR Scheme allowing banks to convert 50% of loans of stressed companies into equities increasing ownership rights of banks in those stressed companies but despite its formalization, the scheme did not resolve the NPA problem or bad loans problem of banks to the expected level.

28

LERMS Scheme under New Economic Policy of 1992

A Seshan, an adviser in the RBI first coined the term LERMS, Liberalized Exchange Rate Management System which was an important part of a reform measure in the transition of (Foreign) Exchange Rate from an officially determined Exchange Rate to a Market based Exchange Rate system in India.

This was part of the Economic Liberalization policies first introduced by the then Prime Minister Mr. Narasimha Rao during the tenure of Dr. Manmohan Singh as the Finance Minister of India during 1992 (New Economic Policy).

Before Market liberalization in India, metrics for import criteria in the Balance of Payments (Refer: Y V Reddy), an officially recorded exchange rate was used which was much lower than the market initiated or market driven rate at that time as was used by other successful and emerging economies of the world.

This was changed after the Economic Liberalization policies of Dr. Manmohan Singh (1992) and shortly after the introduction of the LERMS Scheme during or after the first half of 1992.

As part of this scheme which was called LERMS or a scheme in Current Account Convertibility called as 40-60 scheme on current account convertibility whereas per it, 60% of all receipts on Current account as a result of export proceeds on merchandise could be converted freely into Indian rupees at market determined exchange rate quoted by Authorized Dealers whereas 40% of these receipts on current account were to be surrendered to RBI at the official fixed exchange rate.

This was essentially like the dual rate system which is more similar to Dual price system for let us say sugar whose price as it existed in Open Market was different from what existed in the Public Distribution System.

As we stand today in 2024, Indian rupees is Current Account convertible but not fully Capital Account Convertible.

Current Account convertibility refers to the degree of freedom for a regular Indian citizen to convert let us say Indian rupees into other international currencies and vice versa without any restrictions whenever payments are made in one's current account.

Capital Account convertibility on the other hand is freedom to convert local financial assets into foreign financial assets at market determined exchange rate. This for a regular Indian citizen is only partial. Even though Capital Account Convertibility has advantages such as Ease of Investment in Foreign countries, unrestricted mobility of one's capital and improved access to Global Financial markets, its disadvantages outweigh its advantages in the long run.

Some of the disadvantages may be high volatility of the market which may result whenever let us say a foreign investor exiting the stock markets in India at times when the Federal Reserve in the US increases the Interest rate; also, easier access to Hawala money due to conditions that exist in the Indian Market, a side effect indeed of Full Capital account convertibility if it is allowed in India.

Hence, to summarize, LERMS and its 40-60 policy indeed helped the financial policies in the direction of full Current Account convertibility and partial Capital Account convertibility as it stands today in the Financial Economics world in India spearheading increased business activities in all its realm.

29

A Historic perspective on Quantitative Easing

What is Quantitative Easing?

It is an Economics term used in Financial Economics especially in the administration of Central Banks and Central Banking governance frameworks.

The term actually was in widespread use after the Global Economic crises of 2008 (Lehman Brothers financial crises in the USA followed by the Northern Rock Challenge of the NBFC in UK) its effects were not felt so much in India due to the timely intervention by our Reserve Bank.

However, in many European countries and in the United States, big-name central bank governors were struggling with the challenge of the biggest financial crisis since Great Depression.

Many steps were taken by the US Treasury, Federal Reserve, and European Central Bank including giving updates to Central Banks in the Emerging Capital Markets of the world including China, India, Brazil, Argentina, etc.

During the anxious periods that followed after the year 2008, when prices plunged globally and markets froze, meetings after meeting were conducted by the central banking authorities like People's Bank of China (Zhou Xiaochuan) and by Bank for International Business settlements (BIS), whose sole purpose was to resort to unconventional Monetary Policy which would ultimately control the effects of the global financial downturn.

Now again what is Quantitative Easing?

In other words, Quantitative Easing are a set of measures which are part of Unconventional Monetary Policies.

QE In India

Usually for central banks, the standard and conventional instrument as a matter of policy response to crisis is the policy interest rate.

Once it is brought down as a matter of controlling the crisis situation to zero percentage, and if they find, despite doing that the market is still in crisis they take resort to the so called Unconventional Monetary policies some of which are doing purchases of large-scale assets to flood the financial system with liquidity with the aim of stimulating the economy by repairing broken markets.

In India, Reserve Bank during crisis time has resorted to QE measures such as Rupee-Dollar swap facilities for Indian banks to help them overcome any shortfall in foreign funding requirements, expanding lendable resources to financial institutions such as EXIM (Export Import Bank of India), SIDBI (Small Industries Development Bank of India), and NHB (National Housing Bank), etc.

QE Internationally

Quantitative Easing internationally may include programs which were run by European Central Bank which was Asset Purchase Programs in the year 2014 as well as programs run by US Treasury and the US Federal Reserve which was Interest rate lift off in the year 2015.

What is Asset Purchase Program?

ECB started its asset purchase programs as part of a package of nonstandard monetary policy measures which included nonstandard measures targeting long term refinance operations and consisted of CSPP (Corporate sector purchase programs, (PSPP) Public sector purchase programs, (ABSPP) Asset backed securities purchase programs, etc.

Now What is Interest rate lift off?

Consistent lowering of interest rate by the Fed Reserve might have gotten the policy interest rate to exceptionally low values to the level of zero might warrant a lift off so that the Fed reserve increase the interest rate.

It has actually happened in the year 2015 where the Federal Reserve after making sure the markets regained its ground increased the policy interest rate. It is generally believed that it had a positive impact on Labour Market slack indicating worser unemployment rate, better future wages, and price inflation rate.

30

Capital Structure Theories

Assets of a company when bought with owner's money or equity is termed as Capital and assets bought with lender's money or finance is termed liability.

And hence for any firm, Assets = Capital + Liability.

Hence, Capital structure of a company can be a mixture of Company's common stock or preferred stock which are both equity, and short-term debt and long-term debt which are both Debt.

Capital structure of a firm is decided by its DER or the Debt Equity Ratio and as per Financial Analysts it is a measure of how safe an investment or financing is for a firm.

So, what is DER?

When analysts or financial experts refer to Capital Structure, they indirectly refer to a company's debt equity ratio or DER to see how risky it is for investors or lenders to make an investment in a company or to lend money to a company.

Usually, a company which is heavily financed by debt is riskier and has a more aggressive Capital Structure. And a company which is financed by equity remains less risky or has a low leverage and is moderate or less risky for an investor or lender.

However, a company may take money by leveraging debt from the Capital market because the interest payments that a company make on a debt remains tax deductible and is advantageous for the company, and also, because of the fact that the company may retain ownership rights without any or more of any dilution in ownership unlike equity financing.

Also, at low interest rates, debt may be easily found unlike equity financing which may be hard to get it subscribed.

However, in equity financing the money need not be given back to the owners since he or she already enjoys ownership rights in the company.

To come back to our point, Debt Equity ratio is the ratio of debt to equity in the total proportion of total assets of a company.

For a company, which runs on 40% debt financing and 10% equity financing, we can say that the company is highly leveraged or debt financing is more (40% of debt financing) whereas for a company that runs on 10% debt financing and 40% equity financing, we say, the company is said to have a low leverage (40% of equity financing) since equity financing is more.

Most of the IT companies are low leveraged whereas automobile industries are said to be high leveraged.

One of the goals of the company with debt financing is to find an optimum capital structure (OCS) which is the right combination of debt and equity in its capital structure.

Another topic of interest is Cost of Equity and Cost of Debt?

What is Cost of Equity and Cost of Debt?

Cost of equity is the return demanded by a company's shareholders whereas Cost of Capital would mean costs that a company should pay in order to raise new Capital funds.

In other words, a company's cost of equity is the costs or compensations that the financial markets would require in order for them to own the assets of the company as well as take risks associated with such assets of the company. There are two ways in which normally Cost of equity is found out, one is by

CAPM (Capital Asset Pricing Model) and the other way is by DCM (Dividend Capitalization Model), both of which will not be dealt here.

Cost of Debt on the other hand is the interest that a company may end up paying for its debts such as bonds (Debentures) or issues or loans. There may be differential rates applicable to Cost of Debt before tax and after tax since interest payments on debt are tax deductible.

Since we discussed what is Cost of Equity and Cost of Capital, let us also try to briefly see what is Cost of Capital and Weighted average Cost of Capital?

What is Cost of Capital and Weighted Average Cost of Capital?

Cost of Capital is the minimum return necessary for the company to embark on a capital-intensive project (capital budgeting) like building a factory. Investors and analyst may indicate an investment's potential return by using this term Cost of Capital in terms of its costs and risks.

Companies who may use debt and equity to finance its operations may find itself having more than one source of funds or many sources of funds and assigning weights to these sources of funds in a cumulative way represents what is known as the weighted average cost of capital. Hence, weighted average cost of capital is the average cost of capital from all its sources of funds including bonds (Debentures) and issues which are debt, as well as common stock and preferred stock which are equity.

Capital Structure Theories

Now our topic is to discuss some of the Capital Structures Theories in action.

There are quite a few theories that are in play, whenever one takes a look at this subject: Capital Structure Theories, important ones are,

1. Net Income Approach,
2. Traditional Theory,
3. Net Operating Income,
4. MM Theory,
5. Pecking Order,
6. Trade off Theory and
7. Signalling Theory.

For our current discussion, let us take Net Income Approach and MM Theory.

Needless to say, what has to be analysed is in fact the Capital Structure of the firm in terms of its relations it has to the Value of the firm. Most of the Capital Structure theories are built on this premises. For Instance, the Net Income Approach a Capital Structure theory goes on stating that the Capital Structure changes affect the overall changes in the Value of the firm. Another Capital Structure Theory, the MM Approach or Miller Modigliani Approach goes on stating that the Capital Structure changes have no relationship to the changes that affect the value of a firm.

So, this is the fundamental premises on which the Capital structure theories operate.

To delve a little deeper, we will see namesake what Net-Income-Approach is, a Capital Structure Theory. We will also skim through MM Approach, again a Capital Structure Theory.

Net Income Approach
The capital structure theory known as the net income approach says there is a direct relationship between the capital structure

and the value of the business. That is, lowering the cost of capital can increase the value of a company.

More debt is cheaper because of the ability to deduct interest and lower taxes. Thus, the maximum value under the net income approach is with 100% debt financing.

For example, a company can access debt cheaper than equity financing. Thus, it uses only debt to finance its business and does not issue equity. With the net income approach, the company has lowered its cost of capital to the lowest point with 100% debt financing, which maximizes the value of the company or its Earnings per share since the ownership is not diluted in a 100% debt financing.

As per Durant, as we were explaining, it is understood that Capital Structure changes in a firm affect the total value of a firm. This is because financial leverages or changes in financial leverage (Debt inputs to a firm) overall has an effect on the earnings of the firm which affects the overall value. This theory runs on three major assumptions; of which two of the assumptions we state here which are,

- No Taxes – firm works in an environment where there are no taxes levied.
- Cost of Debt is always less than equity capitalization rate or cost of equity which reflects well in the market drawing relationship between leverage rates and market (capital market functions) which basically draws the relationship between change in firm leverages or debt input levels drawn and its effects on the EPS or earnings per share, considering no fresh equity changes, change to a max.

MM Approach

Next, we will take a look at MM Approach (Miller Modigliani) which in fact is a Capital Structure Theory which states that Capital Structure of a firm imparts no effects on the Total Value of a firm.

MM Approach: Modigliani-Miller theorem (M&M) states that the market value of a company is calculated as the present value of its future earnings, and underlying assets, and is independent of its capital structure. That is, it says, Earnings per share is a function of future and underlying assets and not a function of the DER.

That is no matter if you do take a lot of debt or not, the total value of a firm is left unchanged which would mean the EPS or Earnings per share for the shareholder (earnings for the shareholder) is purely a Capital Market phenomenon and not a question of a firm's Financial Leverage (Debt inputs).

Briefly, the MM Approach states that, the WACC (Weight average cost of capital) of the different sources of funds being acquired by a firm will not change with the changes in the Debt-Equity ratio in the Capital structure or the Degree of Leverage.

Remember WACC is indicative of hidden or otherwise costs of funds acquired which will be at times taken to the balance sheet a firm or indicative of responses DO NOT affect the EPS (Earnings per share). This theory merely states the Degree of Leverage will have no effect on the WACC or in some sense indicative of share values indicative of total value of a firm.

<u>Regulatory Control Measures of the Central Bank</u>

As in any country, India also has a very mature regulatory framework or authority in banking, it is our central bank, which is the RBI (Reserve Bank of India) which regulates the Indian economy and keep its Monetary policy (Money Market) steady or intact and the Indian Capital Market vibrant.

As was explained in the chapter that dealt with Regulatory measures that manages bad loans, the central bank (RBI) through its various measures keeps the bad loans which accumulates in any bank at bay, mainly measures like IRAC (1990), CDR (2000), SDR (2013) and S4A Scheme (2016). In particular, RBI regulatory measures like the SDR (Strategic Debt Restructuring) and S4A (Scheme for sustainable structuring of stressed assets) allow the banks to have equity on stressed companies to the tune of bad loans that they lend to it so that the banks convert bad loans to equity in the financially stressed company.

Most often, this is done through structural changes in the management of the (financially) stressed companies by employing management takeover of them by the bank themselves.

Like in India, in most other countries, this may prompt management teams under the control of banks run the management of stressed companies in other-words a management take-over of stressed companies, which increases the chances to turn around the stressed company to a profit-making phase.

<u>Restructuring Financially stressed companies by banks</u>

After the Management take-over of the financially stressed company, the new management (bank) may introduce financial measures to curb unnecessary expenditure (long term) or expenses (short term) incurred by the company.

It is a matter of observation that in many such stressed companies that is taken over by the bank, the financial structure goes for a restructure, techniques used in most cases may be NIA (Net Income Approach) or MM (Miller Modigliani) though there are a lot of other techniques available to restructure the financial structure in them, so that it helps turnover the company financially.

Here one thing to note is the sensitivity that such an approach presents to the structural stability of the new management (bank) who now runs the financially stressed company. Taking the NIA Approach in financial restructuring poses a problem because the value of the company gets really affected by DER or Debt Equity ratio and it may have an exposure attached to the management structure in question, however with MM Approach that may not be the case. Since many different approaches are available, the turnaround of the company in essentials depend upon a lot of these management techniques that the management employs of what gets going for the stressed concern.

www.ingramcontent.com/pod-product-compliance
Lightning Source LLC
Chambersburg PA
CBHW062229150726
47991CB00006B/2498